# THE TRIAL OF SOCRATES

### BY
### DON NARDO

FAMOUS

TRIALS

Lucent Books, San Diego, CA

Other books in the Famous Trials series:

The Dred Scott Decision
The Nuremberg Trials
The O. J. Simpson Trial
The Salem Witch Trials
The Scopes Trial

### Library of Congress Cataloging-in-Publication Data

Nardo, Don, 1947–
   The trial of Socrates / by Don Nardo.
      p. cm. — (Famous trials series)
   Includes bibliographical references and index.
   Summary: Presents a biographical sketch of this fourth-century Greek philosopher before focusing on his trial and conviction and its legacy.
   ISBN 1-56006-267-3 (alk. paper)
   1. Socrates—Trials, litigation, etc.—Juvenile literature.
   2. Trials (Blasphemy)—Greece—Athens—Juvenile literature.
   3. Trials (Sedition)—Greece—Athens—Juvenile literature.
   [1. Socrates—Trials, litigation, etc. 2. Trials (Blasphemy).
   3. Trials (Sedition). 4. Philosophers.] I. Title. II. Series.
   KL4115.6.S63N37   1997
   940.54'211—dc20                    95-20407
                                              CIP
                                              AC

# Table of Contents

# Foreword

"The law is not an end in and of itself, nor does it provide ends. It is preeminently a means to serve what we think is right."

William J. Brennan Jr.

THE CONCEPT OF JUSTICE AND THE RULE OF LAW are hallmarks of Western civilization, manifested perhaps most visibly in widely famous and dramatic court trials. These trials include such important and memorable personages as the ancient Greek philosopher Socrates, who was accused and convicted of corrupting the minds of his society's youth in 399 B.C.; the French maiden and military leader Joan of Arc, accused and convicted of heresy against the church in 1431; and former football star O. J. Simpson, acquitted of double murder in 1995. These and other well-known and controversial trials constitute the most public, and therefore most familiar, demonstrations of a Western legal tradition that dates back through the ages. Although no one is certain when the first law code appeared or when the first formal court trials were held, Babylonian ruler Hammurabi introduced the first known law code in about 1760 B.C. It remains unclear how this code was administered, and no records of specific trials have survived. What is clear, however, is that humans have always sought to govern behavior and define actions in terms of law.

Almost all societies have made laws and prosecuted people for going against those laws, but the question of which behaviors to sanction and which to censure has always been controversial and remains in flux. Some, such as Roman orator and legislator Cicero, argue that laws are simply applications of universal standards. Cicero believed that humanity would agree on what constituted illegal behavior and that human laws were a mere extension of natural laws. "True law is right reason in agreement with nature," he wrote,

5

world-wide in scope, unchanging, everlasting. . . . We may not oppose or alter that law, we cannot abolish it, we cannot be freed from its obligations by any legislature. . . .This [natural] law does not differ for Rome and for Athens, for the present and for the future. . . . It is and will be valid for all nations and all times.

Cicero's rather optimistic view has been contradicted throughout history, however. For every law made to preserve harmony and set universal standards of behavior, another has been born of fear, prejudice, greed, desire for power, and a host of other motives. History is replete with individuals defying and fighting to change such laws—and even to topple governments that dictate such laws. Abolitionists fought against slavery, civil rights leaders fought for equal rights, millions throughout the world have fought for independence—these constitute a minimum of reasons for which people have sought to overturn laws that they believed to be wrong or unjust. In opposition to Cicero, then, many others, such as eighteenth-century English poet and philosopher William Godwin, believe humans must be constantly vigilant against bad laws. As Godwin said in 1793:

Laws we sometimes call the wisdom of our ancestors. But this is a strange imposition. It was as frequently the dictate of their passion, of timidity, jealousy, a monopolizing spirit, and a lust of power that knew no bounds. Are we not obliged perpetually to renew and remodel this misnamed wisdom of our ancestors? To correct it by a detection of their ignorance, and a censure of their intolerance?

Lucent Books' *Famous Trials* series showcases trials that exemplify both society's praiseworthy condemnation of universally unacceptable behavior, and its misguided persecution of individuals based on fear and ignorance, as well as trials that leave open the question of whether justice has been done. Each volume begins by setting the scene and providing a historical context to show how society's mores influence the trial process and the verdict. Each book goes on to present a detailed and lively account of the trial, including liberal use of primary source material such as direct testimony, lawyers' summations, and contemporary and modern commentary. In addition, sidebars throughout the text create a broader context by presenting illuminating details about important points of law, information on key personalities, and important distinctions related to civil, federal, and criminal procedures. Thus, all of the primary and secondary source material included in both the text and the sidebars demonstrates to readers the sources and methods historians use to derive information and conclusions about such events.

Lastly, each *Famous Trials* volume includes one or more of the following comprehensive tools that motivate readers to pursue further reading and research. A timeline allows readers to see the scope of the trial at a glance, annotated bibliographies provide both sources for further research and a thorough list of works consulted, a glossary helps students with unfamiliar words and concepts, and a comprehensive index permits quick scanning of the book as a whole.

The insight of Oliver Wendell Holmes Jr., distinguished Supreme Court justice, exemplifies the theme of the *Famous Trials* series. Taken from *The Common Law*, published in 1881, Holmes remarked: "The life of the law has not been logic, it has been experience." That "experience" consists mainly in how laws are applied in society and challenged in the courts, a process resulting in differing outcomes from one generation to the next. Thus, the *Famous Trials* series encourages readers to examine trials within a broader historical and social context.

# Introduction

# A Lesson for the Ages

THE SCENE IS A COURTROOM, a spacious hall lined by towering colonnades of graceful marble pillars in the Greek city-state of Athens in the spring of 399 B.C. On one side of the room sits a jury of five hundred men. These jurors constitute the city's whole court of justice, for there are no formal judges, lawyers, or legal officials in Athenian trials. On the opposite side of the room stand several hundred spectators, a tightly packed crowd that occupies every available space in the hall. This highly advertised and anticipated court proceeding has attracted citizens from far and

*A fanciful depiction of the ancient Athenian philosopher Socrates, perhaps addressing the citizen-judges at his famous trial.*

wide, not only from Attica, the peninsula of eastern Greece dom-
inated by Athens, but from many neighboring city-states as well.

Among the spectators are the wealthy Athenian aristocrat
Crito and two of the well-to-do sons of the prominent citizen
Ariston—Adimantus and his thirty-year-old brother, Plato.
These men, along with a few others scattered throughout the
crowd, are close friends of the accused, who stands alone in an
open area between the jury and the audience. The accused is
Socrates, a poor, earthy, old man dressed simply in a loincloth
covered by an unadorned himation, a large piece of cloth
wrapped in folds around his body. His appearance is far from
handsome or noble. He is short and chubby, and his friends often joke with him that he waddles like a duck when he walks.
His markedly snubbed nose has wide, flaring nostrils; and his
eyes, which he has an irritating habit of rolling, are set unusually
far apart. These unattractive features combine with his unkempt
beard and hair to give him what one of his devoted followers
called the look of "one of those Silenus-figures sculptors have on
their shelves." In Greek legends, Silenus was the leader of the
satyrs, grotesque creatures half goat and half human.

But behind this ignoble exterior dwells a surpassingly noble
mind; a powerful, witty, and brutally honest intellect that some
find fascinating and thought provoking and others find disturb-
ing and dangerous. Socrates was known in Athens as a teacher,
thinker, and self-described gadfly, or someone who assumes the
task of periodically "stinging" government leaders and other
prominent individuals with righteous criticism. Now he faces another, less desirable task. Charged by some fellow citizens with
two serious offenses—not worshiping the gods accepted by the
state and community and corrupting the young through his
teachings—he has been summoned to defend himself before
this august, or wise, jury of his countrymen.

As the trial proceeds, Socrates' defense is as unorthodox and
brilliant as his teachings and other endeavors. In a display of
overwhelming logic and insight, he makes fools of his accusers
and shows that the intellectual freedom of the city and its people, including the jurors themselves, is the real subject of the

trial. Nevertheless, for personal and political reasons that go beyond logic, reason, and justice, the jury finds him guilty and sen-
tences him to death. He has a number of chances to escape
either the harsh sentence or the execution itself, but he refuses
to do so on the grounds that such actions would be an admission
of guilt and an abandonment of his principles.

To most Athenians at the time, Socrates' trial and death
seemed justified, but later generations of Greeks and other Western societies saw the event very differently. The verdict of history
has been that the condemnation of so honest and just a man in
what is universally acknowledged as the world's first, purest, and
most open democracy constitutes one of the darkest moments in
the story of human civilization. Nevertheless, out of the shame of
that bleak event something hopeful, constructive, and meaningful
eventually emerged into the light of human consciousness.

*This bust of Socrates, carved after his death, captures his characteristic snubbed nose, widely spaced eyes, and unkempt hair.*

Socrates became a stirring
and heroic example for later
generations of thinkers, writers, artists, and all lovers of
freedom and justice.

As modern scholar Paul
B. Woodruff puts it, "Above
all, he holds a place in history as the first notable martyr for philosophy, the man
who would not renounce
his principles to save his
life." Socrates' pupil Plato
witnessed the trial and used
his mentor, his martyrdom,
and the ideas he died for as
the basis for a new school of
thought, one that pro-
foundly shaped the philosophy, literature, politics, and
laws of all later Western societies. At the core of this

doctrine rests the noble sentiment Socrates imparted to his jurors: "We should not be concerned about winning fame or political honors, but rather should try to gain more intelligence, to arrive at more knowledge of truth, and to develop finer character." These words have become a lesson for the ages.

# Chapter 1

# Growing Up in a Brilliant Age: Socrates' Early Years

V ERY LITTLE IS KNOWN FOR CERTAIN about Socrates' personal life—mainly because almost nothing of a factual and objective nature was written about him in his own time. It is perhaps ironic that this man, who had so profound an impact on later Western literature, philosophy, and intellectual endeavor and was the central figure in one of the most famous court trials in history, left behind no writings of his own. Everything we know about him and his ideas comes secondhand through the writings of others and mostly after he was already dead.

The first literary descriptions of Socrates appeared in the works of his contemporary, the great Athenian playwright Aristophanes, whose comedic plays were widely popular in the second half of the fifth century B.C. In particular, the play

*Aristophanes, one of the four leading playwrights of Athens's golden age, wrote* Clouds, Wasps, Frogs, *and other now classic comic plays.*

titled *Clouds* (produced in 423 B.C.) poked fun at the philosopher by caricaturing him as the manager of an Athenian "think-factory," an oddball and snooty school attended by "airhead" students who passed their days praying to the clouds and contemplating trivial things. Other well-known comic playwrights, including Amipsias and Eupolis, also wrote exaggerated and humorous burlesques of Socrates and his students, but these plays have not survived. Powerful politicians and military generals were the usual butts of such farces and comedians. That a teacher and thinker figured so prominently in the most popular literature of the day shows clearly that he was quite well known and that his ideas were widespread and influential.

The other primary sources of information about Socrates, which appeared shortly after his trial and death, were penned by two of his former pupils, Xenophon and Plato. Xenophon, who gained fame as a military general as well as a writer, produced the *Memorabilia*, a work that defended the philosopher's memory against those who had condemned him during the trial and who continued to condemn him after his death. Plato, a philosopher himself, wrote a series of dialogues, hypothetical conversations in which Socrates appears as a character talking and arguing with various thinkers and prominent citizens of his day. Among the

*Socrates' student and friend Plato, who would, in turn, become the teacher of the great philosopher, scientist, and prolific writer Aristotle.*

more important and revealing of Plato's dialogues are the *Phaedo*, *Apology*, *Crito*, and *Symposium*. Just how many of the ideas and statements attributed to Socrates in these works were actually his and how many belonged to Plato himself is difficult to discern. Many scholars believe that Plato often used his mentor's character as a mouthpiece for his own philosophical concepts. However, no one doubts that Plato was profoundly influenced by Socrates, and a majority of scholars agree that the image of Socrates in these dialogues is probably substantially genuine.

## Witness to the Rise of Athens

From these works by Aristophanes, Xenophon, and Plato, as well as from other assorted Greek historical and literary sources, scholars have managed to piece together a sketchy but presumably reliable picture of Socrates' life and of how his activities led to his famous trial. According to Plato, at the time of the trial early in 399 B.C., Socrates was about seventy years old—placing his birth in about 470. His father, Sophroniscus, and mother, Phaenarete, belonged to the Antiochid tribe, one of ten such tribes into which the population of Athenian Attica was divided. Traditionally, Socrates' birthplace has been accepted as Alopece, one of Attica's many local regions (known as demes), located just south of Athens, although no written records exist to confirm it. According to tradition Sophroniscus was a stone cutter or sculptor and taught his son this craft; however, neither Xenophon nor Plato mention this tale and most scholars now believe that it was based on confused accounts of sculptors bearing similar names. Apparently the mother, Phaenarete, was a midwife who aided in delivering babies in her local community, but little else is known about her. The exact circumstances of her son's childhood remain equally blank in the historical record.

What *is* certain about Socrates' birth and formative years is that they took place in one of the world's most politically and culturally influential societies during its most turbulent, brilliant, and important age. By the year he was born, Athens had already become the marvel of Greece and the most important city-state in the Mediterranean world. Less than a decade had elapsed since the Athenians had gained unprecedented honors, wealth,

and eternal fame after leading the other Greek states in a crushing defeat of the Persians, a west-Asian people who had twice invaded mainland Greece. Inspired by this victory, Athens went on to strengthen its fledgling democracy, the world's first, and to spread its democratic ideas to other city-states. The Athenians also took vigorous charge of a federation of over one hundred Greek cities, the Delian League, and steadily began to turn this alliance into its own self-serving empire.

As a young boy, therefore, Socrates was a witness to and a direct beneficiary of the glorious ascendancy of Athens as the political and economic leader of the Greek world. At the same time, he could not have remained unaffected by Athenian culture—art, architecture, sculpture, and scientific and philosophical ideas—that were also setting the standard for their time (and as it turned out, for all times). The open, liberal attitudes bred by democracy, coupled with the vast inflow of money from Athens's growing maritime empire, attracted artists and thinkers from every corner of the eastern Mediterranean.

## YOU CAN'T ARGUE WITH THE TRUTH

This excerpt from Plato's dialogue the *Symposium* is an excellent example of Socrates' method of asking a series of questions in order to help someone find the truth. After his friend Agathon argues that Eros, a love deity, is the most beautiful of the gods, the philosopher asks, "Is Eros love of nothing, or of something?"

AGATHON: Of something, certainly.

SOCRATES: Good. Hold onto that answer. . . . But first tell me this; this thing which Eros is love of, does he desire it, or not?

AGATHON: Certainly.

SOCRATES: Consider this proposition: anything which desires something desires what it does not have, and it only desires when it is lacking something. How does it strike you?

AGATHON: Yes, it seems certain to me too.

SOCRATES: Quite right. So would a big man want to be big, or a strong man want to be strong?

AGATHON: No, that's impossible, given what we have agreed so far.

SOCRATES: Because if he possesses these qualities, he cannot also lack them.

AGATHON: True. . . .

SOCRATES: Keeping that in mind, just recall what you said were the objects of Eros, in your speech. I'll remind you, if you like. . . . There could be no love of what is ugly. Isn't that roughly what you said?

AGATHON: Yes, it is. . . .

SOCRATES: And this being so, Eros must have an existence as love of beauty, and not love of ugliness, mustn't he?

AGATHON: Yes.

SOCRATES: But wasn't it agreed that he loves what he lacks, and does not possess?

AGATHON: Yes, it was.

SOCRATES: So Eros lacks, and does not possess, beauty.

AGATHON: That is the inevitable conclusion. . . .

SOCRATES: If that is so, do you still maintain that Eros is beautiful?

AGATHON: I rather suspect, Socrates, that I didn't know what I was talking about. . . . I can't argue with you. Let's take it that it is as you say.

SOCRATES: What you mean, Agathon, my very good friend, is that you can't argue with the truth. Any fool can argue with Socrates.

As a boy Socrates probably met and was strongly influenced by many of these brilliant individuals. Certainly, like all Athenians, the youngster must have attended the theater, which had developed in Athens during the preceding seventy to eighty years, and seen the great tragedies of Aeschylus, the world's first great dramatist. Probably making just as grand an impression on the boy was an event that occurred when he was about eight or nine years old: the rise to power of the politician-general Pericles. This great leader, whom Socrates no doubt later came to know personally, led Athens to the height of its power and influence, and posterity has bestowed his name on this brief but glorious period in the annals of Western culture—the Periclean age.

## Soldier and Husband

Only a few of Socrates' personal experiences and endeavors during the Periclean years are known, and none are known in any detail. Evidently he served in the Athenian army on a number of occasions, the first time in 441 B.C. when Pericles led a punitive expedition against the island city of Samos, which had boldly rebelled against Athenian authority. After a months-long siege, the attackers took control of the city, and presumably Socrates then reverted to civilian status. With few exceptions, most Greek soldiers and their military units were citizen militia who responded to a call-up for service during an emergency and then disbanded when that emergency was over.

The next emergency that pressed Socrates into service was a campaign against the city of Potidaea, on the northern coast of Greece, beginning in 432 B.C. At this dangerous time in Greek affairs, Athens, its archrival, the city-state of Sparta, and their respective allies were on the brink of a disastrous war. Although Potidaea was technically an Athenian ally, it had been founded by Corinth, a city that supported Sparta and hated Athens. When Pericles ordered the Potidaeans to break off relations with Corinth, they refused. Pericles responded to this insolence by launching an attack.

During the campaign, reported the later Greek biographer Plutarch, Socrates, then nearly forty, shared a tent with a young

*(Above) The Theater of Dionysus in Athens as it may have appeared in the third century B.C., more than a century after Socrates' death. (Below) A bust of the renowned fifth-century B.C. Athenian statesman Pericles.*

aristocrat in his late teens named Alcibiades, who would one day become a major figure in Greek politics and war. They struck up a close friendship, little realizing that this bond would weigh heavily against Socrates many years later during his trial. According to Plutarch's account in *Life of Alcibiades*:

> There was a fierce battle, in which they both fought with great courage, but when Alcibiades was wounded and fell, it was Socrates who stood over his body and defended him with the most conspicuous bravery and saved his life

and his arms [weapons and armor] from the enemy. The prize for valor was certainly due in all justice to Socrates, but because of the distinction of Alcibiades' [aristocratic] name, the generals were evidently anxious to award it to him. Accordingly, Socrates, who wanted to encourage his friend's honorable ambitions, took the lead in testifying to Alcibiades' bravery and in pressing for the crown and the suit of armor [both awards of valor] to be given to him.

Some evidence suggests that Socrates and Alcibiades fought together again in the Peloponnesian War. That great conflict of the Greek leagues broke out shortly after the Potidaean incident, and the fighting engulfed most of the eastern Mediterranean for twenty-seven years. At Delium in 424 B.C., where Athens suffered a defeat, Alcibiades paid his debt to Socrates by guarding the older man against enemy spears during their retreat.

*This painting on a drinking cup depicts Greek hoplites donning their armor. Typically, they wore cuirasses, or breastplates, of metal, leather, or thick linen; metal helmets of various types; and metal greaves, or lower-leg protectors.*

*Alcibiades, whose life Socrates saved, later became one of the most infamous and hated figures in Greece.*

These references to Socrates' military exploits are important because they establish that he was not always poverty stricken. His familiar image as a poor philosopher who earned no money and had to rely on the kindness of friends for food and other necessities is one that evidently developed in his later years. In the army he served as a hoplite, a heavily armored infantry soldier who fought with a spear and short sword. Because hoplites had to supply their own armor and weapons, which were expensive, historians believe that in the first half of his life, at least, Socrates must have earned a comfortable income, although the source of that income remains a mystery.

It also remains unknown how Socrates managed to support his family once he had become a poor, old philosopher. In midlife, perhaps about the age of fifty, he married a younger woman named Xanthippe, who bore him three sons, one of whom was an infant during his trial. Neither Plato, Xenophon, nor any other ancient writer specified how Socrates fed and housed this family, so they must have lived either on the charity of his friends, as he did, or perhaps on money supplied by Xanthippe's relatives, who may have been well-to-do.

## Facing an Intellectual Dilemma

For Socrates, this major transition from an apparently normal lifestyle to one of poverty, self-denial, and constant searching for the truth and meaning of life was largely the result of a major shift in his worldview. As a young man he had been interested in

science, which the Greeks were the first to study in a rational, systematic way. In particular, a group of thinkers who became known as the Pythagoreans had made great strides in the late sixth and early fifth centuries B.C. toward understanding some of the basic mysteries of nature. For example, following the idea of the scientist Anaximander, who suggested that the earth is finite in size and floats freely in space, they correctly proposed that it is also spherical and just one of many similar heavenly bodies. All of these bodies, said the Pythagoreans, move according to set and provable mathematical principles, rather than by the whims of the gods or other supernatural beings.

*(Above left) A drawing made long after Socrates' death depicts him with one of his sons; and a statue of Pythagoras of Samos, who made important early contributions in the fields of mathematics, astronomy, and music theory.*

Many Greeks, apparently including the young Socrates, found themselves torn between the rational, logical views of the Pythagoreans and the ideas of another group of thinkers, sometimes referred to as the Eleatics. The founders of this school of thought were Parmenides and Zeno. They were not satisfied with the way the Pythagoreans tried to describe natural bodies and events strictly in physical, mathematical terms. Parmenides held that what people perceive as the changing world and universe around them is really only an illusion, a facade hiding an invisible and absolute, or unchanging, reality that humans are incapable of knowing. Zeno concurred in this view and went on to "prove" that traditional mathematics and logic were a mass of contradictions.

Thus, young Socrates found himself trapped in an intellectual dilemma. As his noted modern biographer A. E. Taylor explains, the result of the Eleatics' assault on rational knowledge

> was to produce by the middle of the fifth century B.C. a widespread general skepticism of the very possibility of [gaining] knowledge of the natural world. By the time that Socrates was a young man of twenty the ablest and most outstanding men were all turning away from the physical world as an object of study; it was almost exclusively the second-rate minds which went on patching up the old [scientific] systems. The first-rate men . . . were turning their thoughts in a different direction.

That new direction was to discover and define an effective way of dealing with what people *could* perceive and explain in the world, namely, such things as politics, morality, and the personal conduct of their lives. In other words, since people could never expect to understand the mysteries of nature, they should direct their energies to achieving the "good" and "virtuous" life for themselves and their respective communities. Faced with a choice between the old and new schools of thought, with their often confusing contradictions, the frustrated Socrates eventually decided that he "had no head for the natural sciences" and set his sights on searching for life's truths on his own.

## SELF-KNOWLEDGE VERSUS SELF-DECEPTION

The term "know thyself," which has come to be associated with Socrates' basic philosophy and mission, was originally a simple catchphrase displayed by the Delphic oracle to remind people to accept and adhere to their social stations in life and not to put on arrogant airs. What it meant, therefore, was "know your place." Socrates reinterpreted the phrase in a much more meaningful way to apply to an individual seeking and attaining self-knowledge, as described in this excerpt from Xenophon's *Memorabilia*.

Hereupon Socrates exclaimed: "Tell me, Euthodemus, have you ever been to Delphi?"

"Yes, certainly; twice."

"Then did you notice somewhere on the temple the inscription 'Know Thyself'?"

"I did."

"And did you pay no heed to the inscription, or did you attend to it and try to consider who you were?"

"Indeed, I did not; because I felt sure that I knew that already."

"And what do you suppose a man must know to know himself, his own name merely? Or must he consider what sort of a creature he is for human use and get to know his own powers? . . . That leads me to think that he who does not know his own powers is ignorant of himself. Is it not clear too that through self-knowledge men come to much good, and through self-deception to much harm? For those who know themselves, know what things are expedient for themselves and discern their own powers and limitations. And by doing what they understand, they get what they want and prosper. . . . Those who do not know and are deceived in their estimate of their own powers . . . know neither what they want, nor what they do, nor those with whom they have relations; but mistaken in all these respects, they miss the good and stumble into the bad."

# A New Kind of Teacher

But where could Socrates, or anyone else for that matter, find insights about how to lead a virtuous, useful, and successful life? To gain such knowledge, a great many Greeks at the time were turning to traveling teachers known as Sophists, or "wisdom-sellers." For a fee, a Sophist instructed an individual or group of individuals in various practical subjects, most notably logic and rhetoric, or public speaking, which presumably would increase their ability to get ahead in politics and business and therefore to make money and be successful. The Sophists, many of whom also claimed the ability to teach virtue, became very popular in Athens and other Greek cities in the fifth century B.C.

Despite their popularity, however, Socrates rejected the Sophists. First, he said, their claimed ability to teach virtue was false and misleading, for virtue could not be taught; rather, an individual had to discover it on his or her own. Socrates also objected to the way the Sophists taught rhetoric. Under this system of public speaking and debate, the object was to take a position and then argue it staunchly and exhaustively, no matter whether it was right or wrong. To Socrates, this callous disregard for the truth undermined the very spirit of learning and inquiry.

Finally, Socrates believed that the Sophists' fee arrangement was materialistic and undignified; a true seeker and dispenser of knowledge, he held, should be interested in knowledge and truth for their own sakes and not for the material benefits they could bring. The philosopher passed on this prejudice to his pupil Plato, who in turn passed it to his own student Aristotle. "Sophistry is a hunt after the souls of rich young men of good repute," stated Plato; Aristotle concurred, writing, "The art of the sophist is to appear to be wise without really being so, and the sophist makes money from a feigned wisdom."

Socrates' teaching technique was very different from that of the Sophists. His approach, which later became known as the Socratic method, was to ask meaningful and thoughtful questions about a subject, all the while professing himself to be ignorant of the answers (which was frequently the case). The pupil's series of answers often became a trail leading to a discovery of the truth of the subject as it related to him or her; at the same time, the teacher made his own discoveries about the subject and thus learned along with the students. Under Socrates, therefore, learning was a process of questioning and discussing the natural world and philosophical ideas.

A small number of Athenians and other Greeks found this ap-

*This drawing shows Socrates conversing with some of his followers. Although he had few actual pupils, it is certain that he was acquainted with most or all of Athens's prominent citizens, including the great Pericles.*

proach refreshing and appealing, and over the course of a few years, Socrates gathered a group of followers. These students included Crito, a wealthy friend about his own age; Alcibiades, the aristocratic soldier whose life Socrates had saved; and Plato's uncle Charmides, his cousin Critias, and his older brothers, Adimantus and Glaucon (at this time Plato himself had not yet been born). As his reputation as a wise sage spread, Socrates also became closely acquainted with some of the most notable and powerful Athenians, among them the statesman Pericles; his educated and sometimes controversial mistress, Aspasia; the wealthy businessman Callias; and Nicias, an influential politician in the years following Pericles' death in 429 B.C. Although these prominent individuals did not become the philosopher's students, they were apparently sympathetic to many of his views and activities.

## A Prophet of Virtue

These philosophic views and activities were directed by what Socrates called his "mission," which he had fairly clearly defined by the time he was in his forties. This powerful personal calling

## RIDDLE OF THE GODS

In this excerpt from Plato's dialogue the *Apology*, Socrates recalls the Delphic oracle's famous statement about him being the wisest man and how he struggled to understand the meaning of this divine message.

*The Delphic priestess, known as the oracle, swoons dramatically as she supposedly receives a divine message.*

Chaerephon, as you know, was very impetuous in all his doings, and he went to Delphi and boldly asked the oracle to tell him whether . . . anyone was wiser than I was, and the Pithian prophetess answered, that there was no man wiser. . . . When I heard the answer, I said to myself, What can the God mean? and what is the interpretation of this riddle? for I know that I have no wisdom, small or great. What then can he mean when he says that I am the wisest of men? And yet he is a god, and cannot lie; that would be against his nature. After long consideration, I thought of a method of trying [testing] the question. I reflected that if I could only find a man wiser than myself, then I might go to the god with a refutation in my hand. . . . Accordingly, I went to one who had the reputation of wisdom, and observed him. . . . When I began to talk with him, I could not help thinking that he was not really wise, although he was thought wise by many, and still wiser by himself. . . . So I left him, saying to myself, as I went away . . . I am better off than he is, for he knows nothing, and thinks that he knows; I neither know nor think that I know. In this latter particular, then, I seem to have slightly the advantage of him. . . . The truth is, that God only is wise; and by his answer he intends to show that the wisdom of men is worth little or nothing; he is not speaking of Socrates, he is only using my name by way of illustration, as if he said, "He, O men, is the wisest, who, like Socrates, knows that his wisdom is in truth worth nothing."

began shortly after a fateful encounter with the Delphic oracle, probably sometime in the early to mid-430s B.C. Socrates' friend Chaerephon journeyed to Delphi in central Greece to consult the famous oracle, a priestess (actually a succession of priestesses) who (according to legend) acted as a medium between the gods and humans. People asked questions and the oracle transmitted the gods' answers, often in the form of riddles. "Is there a man in all of Greece wiser than Socrates?" Chaerephon asked. The oracle's reply was "No one."

Socrates was sure that the oracle had spoken a riddle. The answer—that he was the wisest of men—could not really be true, he reasoned, because he knew perfectly well the depth of his own ignorance about many aspects of life. After much thought and investigation, he came to the conclusion that all people, including himself, were ignorant of the most important piece of knowledge—how to "tend" to the soul, to make it as good as possible, and, therefore, to become a truly virtuous individual. The difference between Socrates and everyone else was that he knew what he and they were missing and how important it was to find it. Thus, he decided that the oracle had been right, although in a roundabout way. He was the wisest man, but only because he was intuitive enough to realize how ignorant he was.

Having arrived at this momentous insight, Socrates embarked on his mission. His divinely inspired destiny and purpose, he believed, was to question his fellow citizens about what they knew about life, to criticize them when they erred, and to remind them when they were not being true to themselves. Unlike the Sophists, he did not charge money for his work and gladly accepted a life of poverty. He became, in a sense, a prophet of virtue, a searcher for life's ultimate truths, and in the process he founded a moral philosophy that eventually reshaped Western thought.

At first glance it might seem odd that people in an open democracy like Athens would prosecute and condemn someone for seeking the truth about knowledge and virtue. However, it was not the noble search for truth in and of itself that ultimately led to Socrates' arrest and trial. The problem was that many of

*Socrates (seated at right), a self-professed community gadfly, lectures a group of his fellow Athenians.*

the personal opinions he developed during that quest were un-popular and that he was so uncompromising and outspoken in voicing them. Even in the notoriously liberal and tolerant atmos-phere of fifth-century B.C. Athenian society, Socrates was bound, sooner or later, to get himself into trouble.

# Chapter 2

# Out of Touch with the Times: The Gadfly Makes Enemies

*This statue of Socrates depicts him wearing a tunic as an undergarment and a simple himation hung and folded over it.*

SOCRATES WAS SUCH A UNIQUE IN-DIVIDUAL that he stood out in his community and to a certain degree his eccentric qualities made him an easy target for those who wanted to put him on trial. Though he had his circle of friends and admirers, many people thought him bizarre and felt uncomfortable when he approached. To them, he was a physically homely, strange, and uncouth character who wandered about the streets barefoot, confronting all those who came near him with requests that they examine their souls and defend their views.

His reputation as a meddlesome busybody was not the only odd trait that bothered many of his countrymen. Sometimes in the middle of a conversation he would suddenly become silent, rigid, and stare off into space for several minutes or even for hours, all the while completely unaware of what was happening around him. Modern doctors speculate that he suffered from catalepsy, a condition associated with various physical and psychological disorders, including epilepsy. The ancients thought that such episodes were divinely inspired, making the sufferer seem mysterious, disquieting, and decidedly different from ordinary people. Socrates himself openly suggested that he had been "touched" by the gods and spoke of his *daimonion*, an inner sign or spirit of supernatural origin that made him unique. Supposedly, this inner voice would warn him that certain actions or events would lead to disaster.

Of course, if all Socrates had ever done was roam the streets questioning people and making them feel uncomfortable, he would never have been accused of wrongdoing and brought to trial. No one thought that his peculiar physical, psychological, and social oddities made him a threat to society. What got him into trouble was his strong advocacy of unpopular opinions that clashed with the prevailing political and philosophical ideas accepted by a majority of Greeks. At a particularly turbulent and unstable time in Athenian affairs, his views, which only a decade before had provoked little more than ridicule on the comic stage, suddenly seemed ominous and dangerous to many people.

## Knowledge Is Virtue

One could logically assume that a person who is prosecuted for expressing his or her views must promote a clear-cut and easy-to-understand political or moral philosophy. However, Socrates professed no systematic philosophic doctrine beyond the basic concept that people, including himself, were ignorant of the truth and needed to find it. This does not mean that he had no philosophical views about life; indeed, he did. But they were varied, unsystematic, and often elusive and hard to pin down. This elusiveness was partly because of his teaching style. Instead of overtly preaching his views, he used his peculiar method of questioning, which employed "Socratic irony," or the stance of mock humility in which he pretended not to know the answers. His

*In this detail from a relief on a marble sarcophagus, Socrates speaks to one of the Muses. Daughters of the Greeks' chief god, Zeus, they were the deities who oversaw music, poetry, and the arts.*

technique of intellectual midwifery, that is, helping people to give birth to ideas that they already believed, as opposed to teaching them his own ideas, also frequently gave the impression that he had no set views of his own. "Like a midwife, I am barren myself," Plato has him say. "I have no wisdom in me."

Despite this false modesty, Socrates possessed abundant wisdom, which became apparent on those periodic occasions when he did openly express his views about the human condition. He had a utilitarian, or practical, concept of goodness that was both logical and easily applicable to everyday life. Goodness is not some intangible, abstract quality, he said, but an obvious and useful property inherent in nature. Things that people find useful, that serve a helpful purpose, are both good and beautiful. In his view, even objects that are normally thought of as ugly or repulsive have a kind of beauty if they perform their purpose perfectly. "Is a dung basket beautiful, then?" someone asked him in Xenophon's *Memorabilia*. "Of course," Socrates answered, "and a golden shield is ugly, if the one is well made for its special work and the other badly." In the same respect, he implied, people are good if their thoughts and deeds are useful to the community.

Elaborating further on usefulness, Socrates advocated that nothing is more useful to people and communities than knowledge (by which he meant wisdom, not simple facts); therefore, knowledge is the highest of all virtues. "He who knows the beautiful and good," he said,

> will never choose anything else; he who is ignorant of them cannot do them, and even if he tries, will fail. Hence the knowledgeable do what is beautiful and good, the unknowledgeable cannot and fail if they try. Therefore since just actions and all other forms of beautiful and good activity are virtuous actions, it is clear that justice and every other form of virtue is knowledge.

## The Shepherd and the Herd

It was not Socrates' assertion that knowledge is the highest form of virtue that irritated many of his fellow Athenians. It was instead his belief that only a select few individuals were capable of acquiring meaningful, insightful knowledge, especially self-knowledge. The Sophists, who catered to the masses, openly advocated that all knowledge, including self-knowledge, was teachable; therefore, it could be learned not only by the relatively few wealthy, educated aristocrats but also by the traders, crafts-people, and laborers who made up the majority of the population. Socrates rejected this very popular, democratic view, however, saying that meaningful knowledge was unteachable. It could be acquired only through a process of personal discovery in which a person arrived at a precise definition for knowledge, which was difficult, if not impossible, to do. Consequently, meaningful knowledge was inaccessible to all but a handful of superior intellects.

This idea struck at the very heart of the Greek city-state, or polis, which operated under the premise that even the poorest commoners possessed dignity and that all citizens had a fundamental right to some kind of say in how they were governed. This belief was especially true in democratic states like Athens, where the citizens met regularly in a community assembly to elect their leaders. Socrates seemed to be saying that most people could not hope to attain the wisdom needed for self-government. Therefore, they could not be trusted to govern themselves. In this view a community was a herd that needed a shepherd—a single enlightened individual—to guide it. According to Socrates, the vast majority of people should withdraw from political life and spend their

An Athenian street scene during the Periclean age. Athenians were proud of their democratic principles and institutions and most of them strongly disagreed with Socrates' belief that they could not be trusted to govern themselves well or equitably.

time "tending to the improving of their souls." In this regard, Socrates was no hypocrite. Claiming to be merely part of the herd, he took almost no active part in politics, for which the prominent Sophist Antiphon, who strongly advocated human equality, criticized him. Most Athenians agreed with Antiphon that Socrates' attitude was arrogant and elitist.

Arrogant or not, Socrates' political ideas themselves were certainly far out of touch with the times. He lived in and enjoyed the freedoms of the purest and most open democracy in the world, yet he distrusted and criticized the concept of democracy. Building on his herd-and-shepherd analogy, he concluded that

*A reconstruction of Athens's magnificent Acropolis, which became a symbol of the city's power, prestige, and institutions, including its unusually open democracy.*

## WE ARE ALL BORN THE SAME

Antiphon the Sophist was one of Socrates' harshest critics during the latter years of the fifth century B.C. Unlike Socrates, Antiphon was a strong supporter of Athenian democracy, and as far as modern scholars can tell, the first ancient writer to advocate the Jeffersonian ideal that "all men are created equal." A fragment of the Sophist's essay *On Truth* (quoted here from Kathleen Freeman's *Ancilla to the Pre-Socratic Philosophers*), which was discovered in Egypt in the nineteenth century, disputed the accepted wisdom of the time, namely, that Greeks were innately superior to "barbarians," or non-Greeks. Antiphon wrote:

> We revere and honor those born of noble fathers, but those who are not born of noble fathers we neither revere nor honor. In this we are, in our relations with one another, like barbarians, since we are all by nature born the same in every way, both barbarians and Greeks.

Antiphon criticized Socrates for more than just his opposition to democratic principles as evidenced by this excerpt from Xenophon's *Memorabilia*, probably derived from a real encounter, in which the Sophist chides the philosopher.

> Socrates, I supposed that Philosophy must add to one's store of happiness. But the fruits you have reaped from philosophy are apparently very different. For example, you are living a life that would drive even a slave to desert his master. Your meat and drink are of the poorest: the cloak you wear is not only a poor thing, but is never changed summer or winter; and you never wear shoes or tunic. . . . You must consider yourself a professor of unhappiness. . . . Socrates, I for my part believe you to be just, but by no means a wise man. . . . It may well be that you are a just man because you do not cheat people through greed; but wise you cannot be, since your knowledge is not worth anything.

"it is the business of the ruler to give orders and of the ruled to obey." This authoritarian idea, that most people should be subjects who submit to a ruler rather than citizens who rule themselves, had been rejected by nearly all Greek states centuries before when they had eliminated their kings. Even in the atypical case of Sparta—a virtual police state that had retained its kings—citizens had certain voting rights and a council of elders could overrule a king.

Though out of step with popular politics, Socrates remained adamant. As recorded in Plato's *Gorgias*, he verbally attacked the most revered of the statesmen who had guided Athens to greatness in his own and the preceding generation. These included Themistocles, who had saved Greece by building a navy and defeating the Persians, and the father-and-son military heroes Miltiades and Cimon, all of whom he compared to pastry cooks and called "flatterers of the ignorant masses." Socrates even attacked his friend Pericles, the greatest statesman and democratic champion of the age. The famed leader, charged the philosopher, had made the Athenians "idle, cowardly, talkative, and greedy."

There is little doubt that Socrates ridiculed many lesser-known Athenian leaders in a similar manner over the years. As scholar I. F. Stone puts it in his widely acclaimed book *The Trial of Socrates*, he "used his special kind of 'wisdom' . . . for a special political purpose: to make all the leading men of the city appear to be ignorant fools. . . . He thus undermined the polis, defamed the men on whom it depended, and alienated the youth." While Socrates had every right under Athenian law to criticize his rulers, such attacks irritated many people, made him numerous enemies, and contributed heavily to the negative light in which many of his jurors perceived him during his trial.

## Rocked by Disaster and Crisis

Given that this public prejudice against Socrates, a negative bias encouraged by the lampoons of the comic poets, had been festering for decades, why did his enemies wait until he was seventy to accuse and prosecute him? The answer is straightforward: The political atmosphere in Athens underwent a major change in the years immediately preceding the trial. What had been an unusually open, liberal, and tolerant society, one able to withstand the barbs of any number of critics like Socrates, had become suspicious, fearful, conservative, and intolerant.

This significant political and social transformation was the result of a series of disasters and crises that had rocked Athens in the final years of the fifth century B.C., pushing it from a pinnacle of power and prestige into the depths of defeat and disgrace.

Many Athenians believed that Socrates himself was indirectly responsible for some of the city's misfortunes. For example, the first crisis occurred in 413 at the height of the destructive Peloponnesian War. A popular leader arose and urged the Athenians to send a huge military expedition to the island of Sicily and conquer the Greek city of Syracuse. With the money, ships, and manpower of that powerful city at its disposal, he argued, Athens could easily defeat its longtime enemy, Sparta.

The people agreed with the leader's plan and sent the expedition on its way to Syracuse. But shortly before the troops arrived, the leader turned traitor and joined the Spartans, after which the Syracusans and Spartans annihilated the Athenian force. This treacherous villain who caused the death of tens of thousands of Athenian soldiers was none other than Alcibiades, Socrates' former army buddy. Many Athenians believed that Alcibiades had become the philosopher's ardent follower and that Socrates, an acknowledged eccentric and critic of the state, had somehow corrupted the younger man.

Thereafter, Athens's fortunes continued to spiral downward, and some disgruntled citizens pinned the blame on its democratic government, which they considered to be weak and corrupt. In 411 B.C., a group of four hundred Athenian men, secretly aided by Alcibiades and the Spartans, formed a conspiracy, overthrew the government, and established a tyranny. After only three months the Athenians forcibly removed the

*A much later depiction of Alcibiades, often referred to by modern historians as the "Benedict Arnold of Greece."*

*Spartan and Syracusan hoplites pursue and kill retreating Athenian soldiers during the last stages of Athens's horrendous defeat in Sicily in 413 B.C. Most of the surviving Athenians spent the rest of their lives in hellish slavery in Sicily's stone quarries.*

upstarts and restored democracy, but an evil precedent had been set. In 405, the Spartans crushed the Athenian navy in a battle in the northern Aegean Sea; soon afterward, its resources exhausted and its will to resist broken, Athens surrendered. With the open backing of Sparta, a new group of despots annulled the democracy and seized power. According to scholar Pearl Wilson:

The Thirty Tyrants, as they came to be called, ruled in Athens from September in 404 to May in 403 B.C. Most of them used their power to further their individual aims and satisfy personal enmities. They claimed an intention to purge the city of wrong-doers, and under this excuse arrested citizens and condemned them to death, especially if they possessed wealth the tyrants were determined to confiscate. It was a period of frightening uncertainty. No one could expect justice, and every kind of personal hostility was a constant threat.

## A Paranoid Society

Socrates took no part in this upheaval, for he had long before withdrawn from political life. But the fact that he, who so strongly advocated good and just behavior, did not speak out

*Another of the many later depictions of Socrates. His failure to publicly condemn the Thirty Tyrants made most Athenians suspicious of his patriotism.*

against such injustice surprised many people and made them suspicious. As Stone points out, "The most talkative man in Athens fell silent when his voice was most needed." People were also suspicious of Socrates for another reason. The most prominent and hated of the Thirty Tyrants was Critias, who now joined Alcibiades in the ranks of the philosopher's former followers who had come to no good.

After eight months of terror and death, the freedom-loving Athenians rose up against the tyrants and once again restored democracy. But after years of betrayal, defeat, humiliation, and bloodshed, the Athens that emerged to face the coming of the new century was a pale shadow of its former self. Athenian society at the time can best be described as paranoid, suspicious of anyone who seemed in the least threatening, and anxious to blame and punish someone for its recent troubles. The question was: Who was left to punish? Alcibiades and Critias, widely viewed as the chief architects of the city's misfortunes, were by this time both dead. On the other hand, Socrates, their mentor and a longtime adversary of cherished democracy, was very much alive.

In order to bring Socrates, or anyone else for that matter, to trial, someone had to step forward and accuse him of wrongdoing. Under the Athenian legal system, there was no public prosecutor, nor were there any lawyers. Any citizen could file an official indictment against another, after which it was the accuser's responsibility to try the case and prove the accused guilty.

Eventually, in the year 400 B.C., Anytus, a popular politician who had suffered abuses at the hands of the tyrants and who had helped to overthrow them, instigated the accusation against Socrates. It appears that he wanted to avoid an active role, especially that of prosecutor. Being a wealthy and popular politician, he probably did not want to risk jeopardizing his position, for on the chance that Socrates was found innocent, Anytus might lose his credibility or even become the target of public ridicule. With this in mind, he convinced an obscure young poet named Meletus, who perhaps owed him a favor, to file the actual charges and prosecute the case. Evidently they reasoned that if they lost the case, Meletus had no public reputation to lose. The reason that

### SOCRATES' PROSECUTOR

In this excerpt from his book *The Trial of Socrates*, scholar I. F. Stone offers a thumbnail sketch of Anytus, the man who initiated Socrates' prosecution, along with a suggestion of a personal motive for the act.

Anytus was one of those rich middle-class leaders who disliked full democracy but soon found it preferable to a narrow aristocratic dictatorship—and much safer for life and property. . . . [He] suffered heavy losses when his property was seized by the dictators after he went into opposition [against them]. After the restoration of the democracy, Anytus won respect because he did not use his political influence to sue for recovery of these lost properties. Such suits were barred by the amnesty, and Anytus abided honorably by its terms. . . . [He] himself was not just a master tanner who suddenly became a general in the resistance. Anytus was already a general in the Peloponnesian war; we know he was sent with thirty triremes [warships] in 409 B.C. to take the Spartan stronghold of Pylos . . . but bad weather thwarted the expedition. . . . Something other than politics seems to have aggravated relations between Anytus and Socrates, a disagreement over the education of Anytus's son. . . . It appears that there was a rivalry between Socrates and Anytus for the younger man's devotion. "At one time," Socrates reveals in Xenophon's *Apology*, "I had a brief association with the son of Anytus, and I thought him not lacking in firmness of spirit." Socrates does not tell us what broke off the brief association.

they waited for more than three years after the democratic restoration to make the accusation was that the long war and subsequent tyranny had thrown the legal system, along with many other government institutions, into a state of chaos. Only after Athenian law had been revised and codified was it practical to stage a trial of a major public figure.

## The Charges

The act of accusing Socrates was easy. Much more difficult for Anytus and Meletus was deciding what charges to bring. As they saw it, his crimes consisted of his former associations with the traitors Alcibiades and Critias, his attacks on democracy, and his fail-

## UNDERSTANDING THE CHARGES

In his book *Socrates: The Man and His Thought*, noted Socratic scholar A. E. Taylor searches beneath the surface of the vague and general wording of the charges leveled at the philosopher.

We must be careful not to misunderstand either clause of the indictment. It is certain that the first charge [of going against established religion] does not mean that Socrates holds what we call "heretical opinions," nor yet that he disbelieves the stories of the conventional mythology [tales of the Greek gods and goddesses] as he frequently confesses in Plato's dialogues that he disbelieves them. The religion of the Athenian state was wholly a matter of worship, or *cultus* [consisting of prayer and sacrifice]; it had no theological dogmas and no sacred books. And it is certain that it was no offense against religion to disbelieve in the mythology of Homer [author of the epics the *Iliad* and *Odyssey*] and the poets. . . . The meaning of the second charge, "corruption of the young," is clearer. . . . Socrates is represented by Plato as professing to be much puzzled as to the particular kind of harm he is accused of doing to his younger associates. . . . Reading between the lines, one gathers that what really annoyed Anytus was that the criticisms of Socrates on the incompetence of politicians like himself tended to lower their reputation and to produce a critical [mental] attitude towards the democracy and its institutions among the . . . younger generation, as was certainly the fact.

ure to step forward during the tyranny and oppose the despots. Nevertheless, he could not be prosecuted for any of these acts. Under an amnesty law passed after the tyrants had been deposed, no one (except the tyrants themselves) could be charged with wrongdoing committed during the tyranny or before it. That meant that some other charges would have to be contrived to use against the philosopher. Since Socrates had not overtly violated any laws, the formal charges that ended up being filed were, of necessity, extremely vague and open to interpretation.

The first charge stated that Socrates was guilty of "not worshiping the same gods worshiped by the state." The accusers evidently trusted that the jurors would remember the scenes in Aristophanes' *Clouds* in which Socrates' character declares that Zeus and the other traditional gods do not exist. They also hoped

*A fanciful portrayal of the leading Greek gods (with Zeus on his throne in the center), whom Socrates was accused of rejecting.*

that the jury would recall that shortly before betraying his country Alcibiades had been accused of defacing religious statues. There was no evidence to implicate Socrates in this crime (and in any case the amnesty law forbade calling specific attention to it in the accusation), but some Athenians apparently felt that the philosopher was guilty by association.

According to the second charge, Socrates had "corrupted the city's youth" with his ideas. This charge, of course, was a reference to his old friendships with Alcibiades, Critias, and other discredited characters. Because of the amnesty law, the prosecutors could not refer directly to these associations, so they described Socrates' corruptive influence in terms of "teaching the young to disrespect their parents and the government."

The accusation called for the death penalty if Socrates was found guilty, but it is doubtful that Anytus and his supporters actually wanted to see Socrates put to death. Rather, their aim seems to have been to eliminate him and his antidemocratic influence

*Socrates, depicted here with Alcibiades and Xanthippe, did not flee Athens when he had the chance, but stayed to defend himself.*

during a time when the restored government was still shaky and vulnerable. In fact, the accusers fully expected that after being charged, the self-styled gadfly would quietly leave the city and spend the remainder of his days stinging the leaders of some rival community. But Socrates surprised them by staying in Athens to face trial. As it turned out, the decision both sealed his fate and brought him eternal fame.

# Chapter 3

# Fighting with Shadows:
# The Philosopher
# on Trial

A**FTER SOCRATES HAD BEEN ACCUSED** of wrongdoing, several months elapsed before his trial, for the Athenian courts were typically just as slow moving and backed up with cases as their modern counterparts. Following Athenian custom, he was not arrested after the accusation, but rather was expected to show up in court on a specific date, just as today someone being sued is expected to answer a summons to appear on a given day. Therefore, during this waiting period the philosopher was not imprisoned or restrained in any way. Clearly, he and his family could have escaped quite easily to another city-state, presumably one at odds with Athens, which is exactly what everyone expected him to do.

That Socrates did not go into voluntary exile when he had the chance shows that he had the courage to stand by his convictions. His strictly conservative, authoritarian political beliefs held that the state had the right to question the character of any of its citizens. He believed that a citizen was subservient to the state and that it was his or her moral duty to face the charges brought within the state's legal system. To run away would be, in effect, to abandon the very community that he had devoted his life to serving and improving through his divinely inspired mission.

## The Court Convenes

Consequently, on the appointed day in the spring of 399 B.C., Socrates appeared at court dressed in the same poor outfit he always wore and probably barefoot as well. He must have presented a sharp contrast to most other legal defendants of the time, who wore their finest clothes to court, hoping to impress the jury. Presiding over the proceedings that day, as in all jury cases, was the *basileus* archon, a city official who supervised the court system. His legal functions included ensuring that the charges were properly registered and making all the arrangements for the trial; however, in the courtroom itself his presence was mainly ceremonial, and he had no legal authority as a judge.

*This drawing is probably a fairly accurate representation of the scene in which Socrates confronted his judges.*

The jurors, chosen from the citizenry by lot, or random drawing, were the actual judges. Their job was not only to find a defendant guilty or innocent but also to pronounce sentence. Therefore, they voted twice: the first time for conviction or acquittal and the second, if necessary, to decide on a fitting penalty. There were usually several hundred jurors, mainly so that it would be impractical, if not impossible, for someone to bribe enough of them to influence the verdict. Five hundred jurors were in attendance at Socrates' trial.

The first order of business was for the accuser-prosecutor, Meletus, to state the charges for the record and then to present witnesses who could substantiate those charges. He called both Anytus and Lycon, a professional orator, to testify against Socrates. The actual content of their speeches remains unknown because Plato, who watched from the audience along with some of the philosopher's other friends, did not record them.

Luckily, Plato did set down a record of the next section of the proceeding—Socrates' defense. This document has survived as the famous *Apology*. Though pieced together largely from Plato's memory, and therefore not an accurate word-for-word transcription, scholars believe it is a fairly reliable representation of what Socrates actually said. It is important to note that the Greek legal term *apologia* denoted an accused person's defensive speech, and the word, as Plato used it, should not be taken in the modern sense. Socrates was certainly not apologizing for doing something wrong. Indeed, the situation was just the opposite: He was trying to show that he was innocent.

## Two Groups of Accusers

The long, shrewd, and supremely eloquent speech Socrates gave in his own defense was the expression of a brilliant individual at the height of his intellectual maturity. Using the device of false modesty, as he had done so often and well in employing the Socratic method, he began by insisting that he had no special eloquence as a speaker. Only if eloquence was defined as "the force of truth," he stated, could he be considered eloquent.

*A fanciful depiction of Plato, from a later European engraving.*

The philosopher then claimed that he had two groups of accusers to contend with, the first and most obvious being Meletus, Anytus, and those that sympathized with them against Socrates. The second group, which he feared much more than the first, was made up of many unidentified people who had slandered him and misrepresented his ideas over the years, in the process creating an unfair public prejudice against him. "This class of men are most difficult to deal with," he said, "for I cannot have them up here, and cross-examine them, and therefore I must simply fight with shadows in my own defense, and argue when there is no one who answers."

## OAKS ARE NO LIARS

In his defense, Socrates claimed that much of the unfair prejudice against him had come from the lampoons of comic playwrights, and he singled out Aristophanes' *Clouds*. Clearly, though meant in jest, that play's portrayal of the philosopher as a wisecracking, arrogant Sophist was unfair, for he neither took money for teaching nor professed to know the workings of nature, as the playwright suggests. In addition, Socrates told his jurors that he had never held or discussed any of the bizarre ideas spouted by his character in many scenes in the play. He was undoubtedly referring to scenes such as the one excerpted here (quoted from *The Complete Plays of Aristophanes*), in which the main character, Strepsiades, comes to the philosopher seeking knowledge and is dazzled by the sound of a chorus of clouds, mystical characters whom Socrates worships.

STREPSIADES: O Earth! What an awesome and portentous sound!

SOCRATES: They [the clouds] alone are deities; all the other gods are nonsense.

STREPSIADES: But Zeus on [Mount] Olympus, by Earth, is he no god?

SOCRATES: What Zeus? Don't be silly; there is no Zeus.

STREPSIADES: No? Then who rains? First tell me that.

SOCRATES: These clouds, of course, and I'll prove it by evidence plain. Come, did you ever see rain without clouds? But Zeus [if he is real] should bring rain from a clear sky, when clouds are vacationing.

STREPSIADES: By Apollo, yes; that suits your argument perfectly. . . . But tell me who thunders. Thunder is what makes me tremble.

SOCRATES: It's the rolling of the clouds that makes thunder. . . .

STREPSIADES: But the lightning—tell me the source of its blazing flashes which char or singe us. Surely Zeus firing at liars?

SOCRATES: Fool, you reek of ancient ignorance. If liars are the target why has Simon never been struck, or Cleonymus, or Theorus, liars all? But Zeus' own temple he strikes . . . and the mighty oaks. Why? Oaks are no liars.

Continuing to press the issue of the distorted prejudice against him, Socrates cited the humorous lampoon of his character that Aristophanes had presented in the play *Clouds*. This image of him—a man who claimed to "walk in the clouds" and who spouted "a great deal of nonsense" about natural science—was false and ridiculous, he contended.

> The simple truth is, O Athenians, that I have nothing to do with physical speculations. Very many of those here present are witnesses to the truth of this, and to them I appeal. Speak then, you who have heard me, and tell your neighbors whether any of you have ever heard me to speak a little or a lot on such matters.

He paused for a moment, during which Plato and his other supporters in the crowd must have shouted, "Socrates speaks the truth! We've never heard him discuss such things!" or words to that effect. "You hear their answer," the philosopher continued. "And from what they say of this part of the charge you will be able to judge the truth of the rest."

Socrates then addressed another common prejudice held against him, namely, that he was just another Sophist who claimed to be wise, searched for pupils, and charged money for teaching them. First, he stated, he had never charged anyone money. Furthermore, he had never claimed to be wise; in fact, he had always professed his own ignorance. To prove this, he digressed for a while and told the story about the Delphic oracle: how it had stated that he was the wisest person of all; how he had searched in vain for a wiser person; and how he had finally come to the conclusion that his peculiar kind of wisdom consisted of his realization of his own ignorance. He concluded this story by describing his mission:

> And so I go about the world obedient to the god, and search and make inquiry into the wisdom of anyone, whether citizen or stranger, who appears to be wise; and if he is not wise, then in vindication of the oracle I show him that he is not wise; and my occupation quite absorbs me, and I have no time to give either to any public matter of interest or to any concern of my own, but I am in utter poverty by reason of my devotion to the god.

## The Lone Corrupter of the Community

Next, Socrates turned to what he had called his "first group of accusers," those responsible for bringing the charges against him. The law allowed him to question his accusers, so he called Meletus to stand with him before the jury and be cross-examined. As shown in these lines from the *Apology*, the overconfident poet soon showed that his third-rate intellect was no match for Socrates, who easily manipulated the other man into embarrassing himself.

"Tell me, Meletus, do you consider it important that our young people should become morally excellent?"

"I do indeed," Meletus answered with obvious pride and confidence.

"Then please tell the jury who it is that makes them moral. You must know who it is, since you have made it your concern to discover who corrupts them and in that regard have accused me. Speak. Tell us who it is that improves the morals of the youth." Taken off guard and suddenly nervous and uncertain, Meletus remained silent. "Don't you see, Meletus, that your rather disgraceful silence shows us that you have not given the matter much thought? Speak up, my friend, and tell us who makes our youngsters better."

Utter silence must have gripped the courtroom as the prosecutor struggled desperately for a credible answer. "The laws!" he finally blurted out. "It is the laws that guide their morality."

Socrates immediately rejected this answer. "I did not ask you *what*, but *who*. Tell us the person or persons."

"These men, Socrates. The jurors." Confused, Meletus had decided to fall back on a familiar device used by both plaintiffs and defendants—flattering the jury.

"Do you mean to say, Meletus, that these men here are able to teach our young people good morals?"

"Yes, certainly that is so."

"All five hundred of them?"

"All of them, yes."

"Well, that's good news: that we've got so many teachers of

## MELETUS'S RIDDLE

During his defensive speech, Socrates cross-examined his prosecutor, Meletus. After cleverly leading the man to make the absurd statement that every person in the community except Socrates taught young people morality, the philosopher proceeded to trap him again. This time, as seen in this excerpt from Plato's *Apology* (from the translation by Benjamin Jowett), Socrates got Meletus to say that he, the defendant, was an atheist, which clearly contradicted the wording of the accusation.

SOCRATES: I should like to know, Meletus, how it is that I have corrupted the young. I suppose you mean, as I infer from your accusation, that I teach them not to acknowledge the gods which the state acknowledges, but some other new divinities . . . in their stead. Are these the lessons by which I corrupt the youth?

MELETUS: Yes, I say emphatically that they are!

SOCRATES: Then, Meletus, by the gods, of whom we speak, tell me and the court, in somewhat plainer terms, what you mean! For I as yet do not understand whether you mean that I teach others to acknowledge some gods . . . not the same gods the city recognizes . . . or that I am an atheist simply, and a teacher of atheism.

MELETUS: I mean the latter, that you are a complete atheist.

SOCRATES: What an extraordinary statement! Why do you think so, Meletus?

MELETUS: I swear by Zeus that you believe in absolutely no gods at all.

SOCRATES: No one will believe you, Meletus, and I am pretty sure that you do not believe yourself. I cannot help thinking, men of Athens, that Meletus is reckless and impudent. . . . Has he not compounded a riddle?. . . For he certainly does appear to me to contradict himself in the accusation as much as if he said that Socrates is guilty of not believing in the gods, and yet of believing in them. . . . Did ever any man believe in horsemanship and not in horses? or in flute-playing and not in flute-players? No, my friend. . . . There is no man who ever did. But now please answer the next question: Can a man believe in spiritual and divine agencies, and not in spirits or demigods?

MELETUS: He cannot. . . .

SOCRATES: But you swear in the accusation that I teach and believe in other divinities. . . . Yet if I believe in divine beings, how can I help believing in spirits or demigods?. . . This is what I call the humorous riddle invented by you: the demigods or spirits are gods, and you say first that I do not believe in gods, and then again that I do believe in gods. . . . You have put this into the accusation because you had nothing real with which to accuse me.

morality. And what about the audience here in the courtroom? Do they improve the youth, too?"

"Yes," declared Meletus, confident again and plainly unaware of the trap into which the older man was leading him.

"How about the members of the council [legislature]?"

"Yes."

"Maybe, then, it's the members of the assembly that corrupt the youth; or do they improve them along with the others we've cited?"

"They improve them."

"I see. Then it would seem that all Athenians are improving our youth—with the exception of myself; I am the lone corrupter of the community. Is that what you're saying?"

"Yes!" Meletus snapped. "I most emphatically affirm that you alone corrupt our youth." Despite having been led to advocate a totally absurd premise, the poet held firm and refused to withdraw the corruption charge.

Socrates continued questioning Meletus, all the while making him appear increasingly ridiculous, contradictory, and incompetent. Switching to the other part of the accusation, which alleged that the philosopher worshiped gods other than those accepted by the state, Socrates asked if he was guilty, as charged, of teaching young people not to worship the state gods. Meletus answered that Socrates was indeed guilty of that offense. Socrates then trapped his opponent into calling him an atheist, someone who believes in no gods at all. In a brilliant display of logical reasoning, the philosopher showed that he could not be both an atheist and guilty of the charge against him at the same time. The accusation stated that, while he did not worship the state-approved gods, he did worship "other" gods; obviously if the state accused him of worshiping other gods, it could not accuse him of being an atheist.

## The Defiant Gadfly

Having made a complete fool of Meletus, Socrates dropped the casual, lighthearted tone he had taken since beginning his defense. His confident voice pierced the silence of the crowded hall, and he

*Referring to his role as the community's conscience, Socrates warned the Athenian jury, "You will not so easily find another person like me."*

suddenly became profoundly serious. Socrates boldly told the jury members that he would not cease any activities associated with his mission, regardless of whether they acquitted or condemned him.

Men of Athens, I honor and love you; but I shall obey God rather than you, and while I have life and strength I shall never cease from the practice and teaching of philosophy, appealing to anyone whom I meet . . . to interrogate and examine and cross-examine him, and if I think that he has no virtue in him, but only says that he has, I will reproach him. And I shall repeat the same words to every one whom I meet, young and old, citizen and alien, but especially to the citizens, since they are my brethren. For know that this is the command of God. . . . For I do nothing but go around persuading you all . . . to care most about improving your souls. I say that money does not bring virtue, but rather that from being virtuous one can attain money and many other good things. This is the message that I teach, and if this is the philosophy that corrupts the youth, then I *am* a bad person. . . . Either acquit me or not; but whichever you do, understand that I shall never alter my ways, not even if you kill me over and over again!

At this defiant statement, the onlookers reacted loudly, some of them cheering the defendant, others chiding or booing him. "Men of Athens, do not interrupt, but hear me!" he shouted. "I have something more to say!"

After the room had quieted down, Socrates told his listeners that he was worried about their welfare, not his own. If they condemned him, he said, it would be a sin against God because he was a gift given to the community by God, a gadfly whose task was to stir the "great and noble, but slow-moving state" into life. "You will not so easily find another person like me," he warned, "and therefore I would advise you to spare me."

In order for him to accomplish his divinely inspired task, he continued, he had found it necessary to withdraw from politics, an act that the politically minded Athenians thought suspicious. He explained that he had good reason for doing so: His inner sign had warned him that no politician could do what was right and just for very long. Twice, he recalled, the state had called on his services and in both cases those in power had urged him to commit unjust acts. First, during the great war with Sparta, on the one and only day he had ever served as one of fifty legislators

## A SOLITARY PROTEST

In this excerpt from his book *Socrates: The Man and His Thought*, A. E. Taylor provides details on an incident Socrates cited in his defense—the time the philosopher refused to take part in the illegal execution of some disgraced Athenian generals.

This was the autumn of the year 406 B.C. In the summer the Athenians had saved themselves at the eleventh hour from final defeat by a great naval victory off the islets of Arginsuae, between [the island of] Lesbos and the Asiatic mainland [now Turkey]. But the victory had cost 25 vessels and the lives of 4000 men, many of whom, it was believed, might have been rescued but for the . . . negligence of the commanders. It was resolved to try the generals . . . for their lives, by the process known in Athens as *eisangelia* [in which a person was found guilty or innocent by a popular vote of the assembly rather than by a jury], and the prosecution further demanded that the fate of all the eight commanders . . . should be decided . . . by a single vote. As this was a direct [and illegal] infringement of the normal constitutional procedure, the *prytanes* [a committee of fifty legislators who prepared the assembly's agenda and presided over its meetings; on that day Socrates happened to be one of their number], to their honor, protested strongly, and declared that they could put no such illegal proposal to the vote. . . . After a long and heated discussion, the resistance of the other *prytanes* was overcome by the prosecutors' threat to include their names in the indictment; Socrates remained unmoved, but his solitary protest was [overruled]. The generals were tried and condemned in a body and the six of them who were actually in the hands of the authorities promptly executed.

presiding over the democratic assembly, the citizens decided to execute, in an illegal manner, several generals who had been accused of neglecting their duty. He alone had voted not to take this unconstitutional action and also had refused to change his vote even when some of the prosecutors had threatened his life.

The second incident Socrates cited had occurred while the dreaded Thirty Tyrants had held the city in a reign of terror. He and four other citizens had received an order from the tyrants to arrest a wealthy man named Leon so that those in power could execute him and confiscate his money. The other four, fearing for their lives, had followed the order, while Socrates, unwilling to commit such an act, had simply gone home. His disobedience would almost certainly have led to his own death had the tyrants not been deposed shortly afterward. "I cared not a straw for death," the philosopher told the jury. "My only concern was to refrain from performing such an unrighteous and unholy act." To avoid participating in such injustices, he concluded, he had decided to stay out of politics and public life.

## The Defense Rests

In the last part of his defense, Socrates called attention to certain members of the crowd. "If I am or have been corrupting the youth," he said, "those of them who are now grown up and realize that I gave them bad advice when they were young should come forward now as accusers and take their revenge." He then singled out of the crowd several of his friends and followers, including Plato and Crito. In the interest of discovering the truth, rather than perpetuating the lies contained in the charges, he challenged Meletus to question his former pupils whom he had supposedly corrupted. Not surprisingly, Meletus refused to do so.

*Socrates and some of his students congregate in one of their frequent meeting places—the Athenian agora, or marketplace. At the trial, the philosopher suggested that the prosecutors should question these individuals about what he had taught them.*

"Well, Athenians," Socrates stated in conclusion, "this is all the defense I have to offer. . . . To you and to God I commit my cause, and I hope your decision will be one that benefits both you and myself."

Having finished the *apologia* granted him by law, the philosopher fell silent, marking the end of the first part of the proceeding. It is likely that some of his friends brought him a chair on which to rest, for he had been on his feet for a long time. Friends and followers surrounded him, congratulating and reassuring him, while the members of the jury filed out to consider a verdict. After taking the first of their two votes, these citizen judges would return to decide his fate. If some of them had been surprised by his statements and behavior thus far, they were likely even less prepared for what he had in store for them in the second part of the trial.

# Chapter 4

# A Martyr of the Best Type: Choosing the Penalty

EXACTLY HOW LONG THE JURY took to judge Socrates after he had completed his defense remains unknown. However, assuming that the jurors followed the normal procedure for Athenian trials, we can venture a reasonable guess. It is highly doubtful that juries composed of hundreds of individuals sat down behind closed doors and reexamined and debated the evidence before voting for conviction or acquittal, as is the case today. Strictly from a logistical standpoint, such deliberations would have been too lengthy, confusing, and unruly. As a result, Athenian jurors decided a defendant's guilt or innocence through a simple voting procedure. Prior to voting, each juror received two small, disk-shaped bronze tokens, one with a hole in the center, which stood for guilty, and one having no hole, which meant innocent. The jurors tossed the appropriate tokens into a box or basket, after which four jurors who had been chosen by lot counted the votes. It is likely, then, that Socrates' jurors reached their verdict in a fairly brief span, perhaps an hour or less.

Following customary legal procedure, after a jury returned to the courtroom, one member, also chosen by lot, stepped forward and announced the verdict. If the defendant had been found innocent, he or she was free to go, of course. On the other hand, if the verdict was guilty, the convicted person was allowed to make a speech, in which he or she typically pleaded for mercy and proposed his or her own penalty. Under Athenian law, the jury could not decide the penalty on its own; instead, the jurors chose, through a second round of voting, between the penalty initially demanded by the prosecution and the penalty suggested by the convicted person. Thus, it was possible, and indeed quite common, for someone convicted of a crime to appeal to the jurors' sympathies and thereby to receive an unusually lenient sentence.

What made Socrates' case so unusual was that he did not follow this custom of seeking mercy from his judges. Rather, he remained defiant and true to his principles, even in the face of death. A. E. Taylor has described this scene in the *Apology* as exemplifying "the life of a martyr of the best type, as seen from within by the martyr himself."

## "I Will Assuredly Not Wrong Myself"

The jury found Socrates guilty, which, he professed, did not surprise him. What did surprise him was that the vote was so close—280 to 220. "There are many reasons why I am not grieved, O men of Athens, at the vote of condemnation," he said in the opening of his allotted response. "I expected it, and am only surprised that the votes are so nearly equal; for I had thought that the majority against me would have been far larger; but had only thirty votes gone over to the other side, I should have been acquitted." The philosopher's point that such a small shift in the voting would have been decisive was well taken. Had thirty of the jurors voted innocent instead of guilty, the vote would have been tied at 250 each, in which case he would have been acquitted, for such ties in Athenian courts erred on the side of the accused.

After expressing his surprise at the vote, Socrates proceeded to discuss the nature of his penalty. He began by asking what a person who had benefited the state should expect to get in return: "What would be a reward suitable to a poor man who is your benefactor, and desires only to instruct you?" Many of the jurors must have viewed this as a somewhat arrogant statement coming from a man who had just been found guilty of a crime. Socrates seemed to be saying that he had committed no crime, and in fact, that as an asset to the community, he should be somehow rewarded rather than penalized.

As Socrates continued to speak, he retained this defiant attitude, even refusing at first to demean himself by proposing a penalty.

> As I am convinced that I never wrong another, I will assuredly not wrong myself. I will not say to myself that I deserve any evil, or propose any penalty. Why should I? Because I am afraid of the penalty of death which Meletus proposes? When I do not know whether death is a good or evil, why should I propose a penalty which would certainly be evil? Shall I say imprisonment? And why should I live in prison, and be a slave of the city officials? Or shall the penalty be a fine, and imprisonment until the fine is paid? I have the same objection for this. I should have to lie in prison, for I have no money and cannot pay. And if I say exile . . . I must indeed be blinded by the love of life, if I am so irrational as to expect that when you, who are my own countrymen, cannot endure my lectures and words . . . others are likely to endure me. . . . And what a life should I lead, at my age, wandering from city to city, ever changing my place of exile and always being driven out!

*Socrates explained to the jurors that for him, exile, a life of wandering from one foreign city to another, was not a realistic option.*

Explaining his last remark, he said that no matter where he went, young men would surely flock to hear and learn from him, just as they had in Athens. If he refused to associate with them, they would angrily demand that their parents drive him away. On the other hand, if he offered to teach the young men, as he had done in Athens, the parents would drive him away out of fear that he might be corrupting their children. No matter what he did, someone would drive him away. Clearly, then, for him exile was a no-win situation and therefore not a viable option.

## To Pay a Fine?

In the conclusion of his speech Socrates finally relented a little and suggested a penalty. For want of a better alternative, he proposed paying a fine; but because he had no money, he asked that the fine be small and indicated that the sum of one *mina* seemed appropriate to him. At the time, a *mina* was a monetary measure worth one hundred drachmas and one drachma was about enough to purchase a bushel of grain. Presumably, with a *mina* one could buy a hundred bushels of grain, enough to make a great many loaves of bread.

Of course, to someone as poor as Socrates even this modest sum was a lot of money, and he would have to borrow it from his friends. In fact, he acknowledged that some of these friends, namely, Plato, Crito, Critobulus, and Apollodorus, fearing that a fine of a single *mina* would not satisfy the jury, had offered to loan him thirty *minae*. "Very well, then," he said, concluding his speech, "let the penalty be thirty *minae*, and the good credit of my friends will be your assurance that the sum will be paid."

The defendant's penalty proposal having been made, the jurors once again retired to vote. When they returned, the news was not good for Socrates. They had chosen the death penalty, as originally proposed by Meletus, and this time the voting margin was significantly wider than before—360 to 140.

It is not difficult to guess why so many more jurors turned against Socrates after he had delivered his second speech. They must have been surprised and angered by his lighthearted and unrepentant tone, which they interpreted to mean that he did not take the charges, the trial, or the jury itself very seriously. The de-

## PROPHECY OF A CONDEMNED MAN

In his third and final speech in the courtroom, Socrates addressed his enemies. This excerpt from Plato's *Apology* contains Socrates' prediction that by killing him the jury would leave themselves open to eventual harsh criticisms and denunciations leveled by those who sympathized with him and his ideas.

And now, O men who have condemned me, I will gladly make a prophecy; for I am about to die, and in the hour of death [according to superstition] men are gifted with prophetic power. And I prophesy to you who are my murderers, that immediately after my departure punishment far heavier than you have inflicted on me will surely await you. You have killed me because you wanted to escape me, your chief critic, and not to give an account of your lives. But that will not be as you suppose: to the contrary. For I say that you will have to contend with many more critics than you do now; critics who, before this, I have restrained: and as they are younger, they will be more inconsiderate with you, and you will be more offended by them. If you think that by killing men you can prevent someone from criticizing your evil lives, you are mistaken; that kind of escape is neither possible nor honorable; the easiest and the noblest way is not to be tearing down others, but to be improving yourselves. This is the prophecy which I pronounce before my departure to the judges who have condemned me.

fendant's proposal to pay a fine was likely also seen as a sign of arrogance and a gesture of disrespect for the jury and the legal system in general. Though vaguely worded, everyone agreed that the charges fell under the guidelines of the crime of sacrilege, which was normally a capital offense punishable by death. Most (although certainly not all) people viewed a fine as too lenient a penalty for a capital crime.

Although they believed a fine was too lenient, most jurors would probably have been willing to reduce the death sentence to imprisonment or exile, both of which would have satisfied the prosecutors, whose main aim was only to remove the elderly gadfly from Athenian society. All the philosopher would have had to do was to follow custom—that is, admit his guilt and throw himself on the jury's mercy. Instead, he had knowingly and openly provoked the jurors.

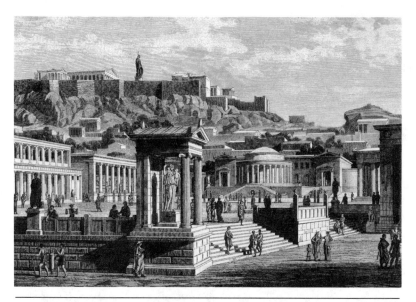

*The Athenian agora, or marketplace. Even here, in the heart of local commerce, thirty* minae, *equivalent to three thousand drachmas, was a considerable sum. If Socrates had originally proposed this as his fine, his jury might have spared him.*

Most insulting of all in the eyes of many jurors was the relatively trivial amount of the fine that Socrates first proposed to pay—one *mina*. Without doubt, those who had voted him guilty in the first ballot would have considered this sum far too inadequate a penalty for the crimes involved. Apparently, even some of those who had first voted to acquit him had agreed and turned against him. Even though he increased the sum to thirty *minae* in the end, the damage had already been done. As I. F. Stone puts it:

> Had the thirty-*minae* fine been proposed by Socrates originally, it might have seemed enough to a jury as closely divided as his was on the vote for conviction. But the first . . . counterpenalty offered by Socrates [payment of one *mina*] must have made the jury feel he was laughing at them, and treating the trial with contempt, as indeed he was. This must have made the final, and reluctant, offer of thirty *minae* too late to appease the jury.

## Immorality Runs Faster than Death

After the death sentence was pronounced, Socrates spoke one last time to the crowd in the courtroom. He divided these remarks—the condemned man's final words, a privilege still granted in many trials today—into two sections. The first, directed at those who had condemned him, was as defiant, uncompromising, and unafraid as his earlier speeches.

> Not much time will you gain, O Athenians, in return for the evil name which you will get from the city's critics, who will say that you killed Socrates, a wise man; for they will call me wise, even though I am not wise, when they want to shame you. If you had waited a little while, your desire would have been fulfilled in the course of nature. For I am far advanced in years, as you may perceive, and not far from death. . . . I do not repent of the style of my defense; I would rather die after having spoken in that way, than speak the way you do and live. . . . The difficulty, my friends, is not to avoid death, but to avoid immorality; for that runs faster than death. I am old and move slowly, and the slower runner [that is, death] has overtaken me, while my accusers are keen and quick, and immorality, an even faster runner, has overtaken them.

*Another of the many later depictions of Socrates addressing his judges. Killing him, he warned, would be an immoral act they would come to regret.*

## DEATH A GOOD THING?

In their book *Plato's Socrates*, two noted philosophy professors, Thomas C. Brickhouse and Nicholas D. Smith, discuss Socrates' remarks about death in the last speech he made at his trial. This excerpt illustrates how modern scholars analyze ancient writings to discover what motivated the people of those times.

Only twice in Plato's early dialogues does Socrates discuss in detail what he thinks death might be like. One of those two passages occurs [in the] *Apology*, where Socrates attempts to console those of his jurors who voted for his acquittal. Though it has now become clear that he will be executed, Socrates has become convinced that his death will be no evil, for he says "a wonderful thing has happened": his *daimonion* [inner voice], which would surely have opposed him if what he was doing was leading him astray, has never once interrupted him the entire day. From this, Socrates feels confident that the outcome of his actions—including the sentence of death—is a good thing for him. Even if we suppose that Socrates' inference in this case is sound, this "great proof," as he calls it, that his death will be no evil, does not guarantee that death in general will be no evil. If it did, our problem would be solved, for then any evil life would be a fate worse than death. But Socrates' "great proof" only shows (at most) that Socrates' *own* death will be no evil; nothing is implied about what might be in store for other people by his *daimonion*'s silence, a fact of which Socrates is well aware. As Socrates leaves the courtroom, he makes this final remark: "I go to die, and you to live; but which of us goes to the better thing is clear to none but the god." For all he can say based on his "great proof," his own death will not be an evil for him precisely because death is never an evil. But it may also be the case that death offers very different possibilities for different people. Thus, whatever Socrates' degree of confidence that his own death will be no evil for him, it may well be that the jurors' lot in continuing to live will nevertheless be better than the lot awaiting Socrates in death. If so, death would be at least a relative evil for his jurors, since for them it would be a fate worse than life. Socrates supposes that his own death will be a boon, for he suspects that if he were to go on living his life would be a troubled one.

Socrates' skillful use of the metaphor about the runners was a poetic way of saying that although he could not avoid death, those who had accused and condemned him could not escape the fact the killing him was an immoral deed.

The philosopher continued to develop this theme—that his enemies were wrongdoers—by predicting that they would ultimately suffer far worse punishments than he. Calling them murderers, he said that they were killing him in order to silence their worst critic; however, he prophesied that many more such critics would follow him and that these younger men would offend the citizens far more than he ever had.

## The Hour of Departure

Socrates' stern tone and serious manner now abruptly changed as he began to address his friends and supporters, who probably crowded in around him. "Friends," he said, "I would like also to talk with you . . . before I go to the place at which I must die." Seeing the deep concern and sadness on their faces, he attempted to console them with the following incomparably beautiful insight into the nature of death.

> Let us reflect . . . and we shall see that there is great reason that death is a good thing: for one of two reasons—either death is a state of nothingness and utter unconsciousness, or, as men say, there is a change and migration of the soul from this world to another. Now, if you suppose that there is no consciousness, but a sleep like the sleep of him who is undisturbed even by dreams [and therefore enjoys totally restful slumber], death will be an unspeakable gain . . . for eternity is then only a single night. But if death is the journey to another place, and there, as men say, all the dead abide, what good . . . can be greater than that? . . . I shall then be able to continue my search into true and false knowledge; as in this world, so also in the next; and I shall find out who is wise, and who pretends to be wise, and is not. . . . In another world they do not put a man to death for asking questions: assuredly not. For besides being happier than we are, they will be immortal. . . . Be of good cheer about death, and know of a certainty that no evil can happen to a good man, either in life or after death.

After talking with his supporters a while longer, Socrates saw that some court-appointed guards stood waiting to take him to a prison cell. "The hour of departure has arrived," he told his friends, and we go our separate ways—I to die, and you to live. Which of these is better, only God knows." We do not know for sure how he bore himself as they led him away, for Plato did not record this detail; however, we can confidently surmise that even in this moment of tremendous adversity, Socrates displayed the same serenity and dignity that had been the consistent hallmarks of his character.

# Chapter 5

# The Best, Wisest, and Most Just: Socrates' Last Days

W HEN THE GUARDS LED SOCRATES away from the courtroom, most of his friends no doubt believed that they would never see him again. They knew that under Athenian law the normal procedure in capital cases was to execute a condemned person within twenty-four hours of the passing of the sentence. To their

*This building in Athens is thought to be the prison in which Socrates spent his final days.*

## PUNISHMENT IN ANCIENT ATHENS

The second half of Socrates' trial, as in other Athenian court trials, was concerned with choosing an appropriate penalty. The jury voted to select either the penalty called for by the prosecutor, which was usually the one prescribed by law, or the one the defendant had proposed. The charges against Socrates technically fell under the heading of sacrilege; along with murder, treason, and a handful of other offenses, this particular crime was punishable by both confiscation of property and death.

The method of execution varied considerably, depending on the social status of the condemned. For example, a free Athenian citizen was usually accorded the privilege of a nearly painless death, most often the drinking of a potion of hemlock, a poison plant, which slowly numbed the body parts until it reached the heart. This, of course, is how Socrates met his end. By stark contrast, slaves, especially rebellious ones, were often beaten to death with clubs. Many condemned persons avoided trial, execution, or both by voluntarily abandoning their property and going into exile, a practice commonly accepted for citizens but frowned on for slaves.

The penalties for lesser crimes also varied. For most minor offenses, citizens generally received fines, some of which could be stiff, or had to give up some of their property, whereas slaves were most often flogged or branded. This followed an ancient general principle of Greek law—that a free citizen should be punished in his property, but a slave in his body. Imprisonment was only rarely used for either citizens or slaves, partly because housing and feeding a regular prison population was costly and widely viewed as a waste of state funds.

relief, however, they discovered that the philosopher's case constituted an unusual exception. It so happened that the day before his trial was also the beginning of a special Athenian ritual.

According to legend, the Athenians had once been forced annually to send several children to the island kingdom of Crete, there to be sacrificed to a horrible monster who was half man and half bull. Eventually, the Athenian hero Theseus put a stop to the practice by killing the monster. To celebrate this deliverance, each year Athens sent a sacred boat to the island of Delos, in the center of the Aegean Sea, to give thanks at the shrine of Apollo, god of light, healing, and inspiration. Before the boat was dispatched, Athens underwent a ritual of religious purification; consequently, the period during which the delegation was away was seen as holy. No executions could be carried out during this period, which meant that Socrates would remain alive until the sacred vessel returned.

In the meantime, the authorities placed Socrates in a prison cell. His wealthy friend Crito tried to persuade them to allow the philosopher his liberty while awaiting execution. Crito offered to supply any necessary security against an escape attempt, but his efforts were in vain. In fact, the authorities kept Socrates chained in the prison—a precaution that most people viewed as unnecessary and cruel. Nevertheless, the prisoner was allowed daily visits from his family and friends. Because the sacred boat was unexpectedly detained, he was able to enjoy a month of his usual penetrating dialogues with his devoted followers, some of whom journeyed from other cities and remained in Athens while Socrates was imprisoned.

*In his prison cell, Socrates and friends discuss the immortality of the human soul.*

## A Contract with the Laws

Sometime during that fateful month, Socrates' friends made a last attempt to save him. Without his knowledge, they made preparations for his escape, including obtaining necessary moneys from some of his admirers in the city-state of Thebes, north of Athens, and bribing the guards to look the other way at the crucial moment. But when informed of the plan, the condemned man refused to take part. His rationale was similar to the one he had cited when he had refused to go into voluntary exile while awaiting trial. Running away, he maintained, would constitute an abandonment of both his country and his convictions.

In his dialogue the *Crito*, Plato recorded in considerable detail the way Socrates expressed this rationale to Crito, who was probably the main instigator of the escape plan. Waking from a deep sleep in his prison cell, the philosopher was surprised to see his longtime friend sitting near his bed. "Tell me, Crito, how in the world did the guard happen to let you in at this early hour?"

"He's used to me, Socrates. Besides, I often give him something."

"Why did you come to visit so early? Has the ship arrived at last from Delos?"

"Not yet. But it will be here soon enough. Listen to me, Socrates! There is still time to save you! Simmias has come from Thebes in Boeotia, bringing plenty of money for your escape. His friend Cebes will also contribute, as will many others."

The older man, his demeanor causal and gentle, replied:

My dear Crito, let us consider this matter carefully. I can't so easily cast aside the principles I have held highest all my life. I have always been the kind of man who is guided by logical reasoning. Let us consider now whether it would be right for me to escape. We have always maintained that one should never do wrong, not even to people who have done him wrong, haven't we? Were we wrong in saying so? Isn't injustice always evil and disgraceful?

"It is, of course," replied Crito.

Socrates continued:

Imagine that just when I was beginning my escape the city's laws, suddenly endowed with form and voice, stood before me and demanded, "Just what do you think you're doing, Socrates? Apparently you are planning to destroy us to the best of your ability. For can a government continue to exist in which legal decisions have no strength, but can be overthrown by any person at will?" I might answer them that I was justified in escaping because the government had imposed on me an unfair sentence.

"Yes!" declared Crito emphatically. "You *could* rightly claim that." To which Socrates replied:

But the laws might continue, "Your parents were married according to us, the laws of Athens, and under us you were well educated. In a sense, then, you are our child as much as you are your father's son. When you went into battle for us and for your country, you accepted the chance of death. The same holds true in a court of law: you must do as your country orders. Any Athenian who does not like the laws is always free to go to another Greek state, taking all his property. So a person who stays here has entered into a kind of contract, agreeing to do what we command. If you escape now, you will prove that you are nothing more than a corrupter of the law, and therefore likely to corrupt the people, both young and old." These are the words I keep hearing, Crito. So you see, you needn't waste your breath trying to convince me to escape. Let us accept things as they are, since it is God's will.

## The Day Most Dreaded

Resigned to the fact of his death, Socrates' friends gave up their plotting and tried their best to enjoy their daily visits with him. Inevitably, the day they most dreaded eventually arrived; news came early in the morning from Piraeus, Athens's port town, that the sacred ship had returned from its mission to Delos. The execution could now proceed, which involved drinking poison, although custom allowed the condemned man to put it off until late in the day.

*Athens's port town of Piraeus (note the Athenian Acropolis rising in the distance), where the sacred ship docked on its return from its mission to the island of Delos.*

In the morning of that last day, the philosopher's followers, except for Plato, who was ill, appeared in the prison to bid him farewell. The nature of Plato's illness is unknown, but it is certainly plausible that emotional distress over his friend's impending demise had incapacitated him. In any case, Plato later closely questioned some of those who were present and recorded the day's events in the *Phaedo*. The dialogue was named after one of Plato's friends, a young man deeply devoted to Socrates, whom the author assigns the role of narrator in the piece. According to this account, Socrates' last visitors included Crito, Crito's son Critobulus, and Phaedo, of course, along with Apollodorus, Aeschines, and a few other Athenians. Also present were the Thebans Simmias and Cebes, who had helped plan the would-be escape, and two of the philosopher's admirers from the city-state of Megara.

When these men entered the cell, they found that Socrates had just been released from his chains. He was comforting his wife, Xanthippe, who was weeping, and their youngest son, both of whom apparently had spent the night with him. After some of the visitors led her away, perhaps to compose herself, Crito and the others sat down with the philosopher and a discussion ensued.

At first they engaged in some small talk about Aesop's fables, the famous morality tales penned more than a century before, which Socrates had been reading in prison. Cebes said that the well-known poet Evenus had heard that the condemned man was writing poems based on these fables and wondered why he was trying his hand at writing for the first time. "Tell him,"

*While awaiting death in prison, Socrates tries his hand at writing. Unfortunately, no documents attributed to him have survived.*

Socrates replied, "that I have no intention of competing with him as a poet, which would be no easy task!" He went on to explain that he had recently had a dream in which he had received the advice to compose music, which one might interpret as poetic verses. So, he said, "I took some fables of Aesop, with which I was familiar, and tried turning them into verse."

## The Mortal and the Immortal

Not surprisingly, the discussion soon drifted to topics relating to the current situation, including suicide and death. With their friend's untimely end only hours away, Cebes and Simmias eventually expressed their concerns about the nature of the human soul. The unemotional scientific explanation, they said, was obviously that when a person died the soul simply dissipated into the air and, therefore, was not immortal. Cebes spoke:

Some people fear that when the soul has left the body its

place may be nowhere, and that on the very day of death it may perish and come to an end—right after release from the body, dispersing like smoke or air and vanishing away into nothingness.

Socrates immediately accepted this as a fitting topic for discussion, since he would soon discover for himself whether or not the soul was eternal. He began:

Shouldn't we attempt to define the thing you fear so much may be scattered and lost? And then inquire further whether what actually disperses after death is the soul or something else? Let us suppose that there are two sorts of existences—one seen and the other unseen.

"Very well," said Cebes. "Let us suppose them."

"Would you agree that the seen is the changing, and the unseen is the unchanging?"

"Yes."

"And further, is not one part of us body, another part soul?"

"Absolutely," Cebes answered.

"And is the soul seen or not seen?"

"No man can see it, Socrates."

To which Socrates responded:

Very well. Now consider this: when the soul and the body are united, then nature orders the soul to rule and govern, and the body to obey and serve. Now, which of these two functions is akin to the divine? and which to the mortal? Doesn't the divine appear to you to be the one that naturally orders and rules, and the mortal the one that is subject to and serves it? Which of the two does the soul resemble?

"It resembles the divine," said Cebes, "and the body resembles the mortal—there's no doubt about it, Socrates."

Socrates asked in conclusion:

Then, isn't this the answer we're looking for?—that the

soul is like the divine, and immortal, and intellectual, and uniform, and unchangeable; and that the body is mortal, and unintellectual, and changeable?

And is it likely that the soul will be blown away and destroyed immediately after leaving the body? That can never happen, my dear Simmias and Cebes. I say that the soul, itself invisible, departs for the invisible world—to the divine and immortal and rational realm, released from the error and folly of men, their fears and wild passions and all other human ills, and dwells forever in the company of the gods.

### A NEW CONCEPT OF THE SOUL

Much of the discussion in Socrates' cell on the last day of his life centered on the nature of the human soul, or *psyche*. Here, from his book *The Philosophy of Socrates*, scholar Norman Gulley comments on how Socrates played an instrumental role in the development of the concept of the soul as an immortal entity.

Much has been written about the development which took place in the Greek concept of the soul in the two centuries before Socrates. . . . The position in the latter half of the fifth century B.C. was that the concept of the *psyche*, while it had been examined and developed within the materialistic [philosophies] of the pre-Socratics [philosophers who lived before Socrates], had attracted no serious philosophical attention as a non-naturalistic concept [that is, thinkers saw the soul in scientific terms—as a physical force that animated a person but did not survive after death]. . . . Socrates was no doubt familiar with these developments. . . . We must now consider, in relation to these influences, how much originality there is in the Socratic concept of the soul. . . . In Xenophon's *Memorabilia* Socrates says that the soul is the most excellent part of a man, and that it is that in him which "partakes of the divine." Elsewhere in the *Memorabilia* he emphasizes the dualism of soul and body in a way which implies that for him the soul is incorporeal [separate from the body]. Unlike the body, the soul is invisible. It directs the body. And it is because it is the seat of reason and intelligence that it is able to do this; for it is in the soul alone that intelligence resides. Moreover, a person's *moral* behavior is the behavior of his soul, not his body. . . . It is essentially the Socratic concept of the soul which Plato attempts to justify in the *Phaedo*.

*Socrates converses with his friends as the jailer, bearing the fatal dose of poison, looms near.*

## The Last Hour

The philosopher and his friends continued their discussion for a long while, touching on many other interesting points about the soul, immortality, and the afterlife. Finally, with sunset approaching, Socrates excused himself and retired to an adjoining chamber, where he bathed and had a last private meeting with his wife and children. Then he returned to Crito, Cebes, and the others.

A few minutes later, the jailer entered. The trembling man, who had come to know and greatly to admire Socrates in the preceding month, called him "the noblest, gentlest, and best of all who ever came to this place." The jailer begged the philosopher not to blame him for his part in the unhappy duties the authorities

## LIKE ANTS AND FROGS AROUND A MARSH

Among the topics Socrates and his friends supposedly discussed on the day of his death was the nature of the earth. In this excerpt from Benjamin's Jowett's translation of Plato's *Phaedo*, the philosopher hypothesizes that the earth is a sphere floating freely in space. Whether the real Socrates actually advocated this view, which was influenced by earlier Greek thinkers, or Plato advocated it and used his mentor as a mouthpiece remains unclear.

My conviction is that the earth is a round body in the center of the heavens, and therefore has no need of air or any other similar force to support it, but is kept there and hindered from falling . . . by the uniformity of the surrounding heaven and by its own equipoise [even distribution of weight]. . . . Also I believe that the earth is very vast, and that we who dwell in the region [of the Mediterranean Sea] inhabit only a tiny portion about the sea, like ants or frogs around a marsh, and that there are other inhabitants of many other like places; for everywhere on the face of the earth there are hollows of various forms and sizes, in which the water and the mist and the lower air collect. But the true earth is pure and situated in the pure heaven— there are the stars also; and it is the heaven which is commonly spoken of by us as the ether, and of which our own earth is the sediment gathering in the hollows beneath.

had assigned him, namely, the imprisonment and execution. Before Socrates could respond, the man, overcome with emotion, burst into tears and ran out. Not long afterward, one of the jailer's attendants entered, bearing the instrument of death—a cup of poison hemlock. When the old man asked him what he should do after drinking the potion, the attendant answered, "You have only to walk about until your legs are heavy, and then to lie down, and the poison will act."

Taking the cup, Socrates raised it to his lips while his friends, their bodies frozen in dreadful anticipation, their expressions pale and anguished, looked on. Then, according to Phaedo in Plato's account, "without the least fear or change of color or feature, he quite readily and happily drank the poison." This action unleashed a sudden flood of emotion from the onlookers. "Before this," Phaedo continued, "most of us had been able to control our sorrow, but now, seeing him drinking, we could no longer hold

## THE NOBLEST DEATH

Besides Plato's *Phaedo*, the other important ancient source about Socrates' last days is Xenophon's *Memorabilia*. Because Xenophon was not present at the time of the philosopher's trial and death and penned the *Memorabilia* many years later, he had to rely for information on sketchy, secondhand accounts. Consequently, this passage from the work is less a record of events and more a fond remembrance of Socrates' character.

> There is no record of a death more nobly borne. For he was forced to live for thirty days after the verdict was given, because it was the month of the Delia, and the law did not allow any public execution to take place until the sacred delegation had returned from Delos. During this interval, as all his intimate friends could see, he continued to live exactly as before; and, in truth, before that time he had been admired above all men for his cheerfulness and serenity. How then, could someone die more nobly? Or what death could be nobler than the death nobly faced? . . . For myself, I have described him as he was: so religious that he did nothing without counsel from the gods; so just that he did no injury, however small, to any person, but conferred the greatest benefits on all who dealt with him; so self-controlled that he never chose the pleasanter rather than the better course; so wise that he was unerring in his judgment of the better and the worse . . . masterly in putting others to the test, and convincing them of error and urging them to follow virtue and gentleness. To me, then, he seemed to be all that a truly good and happy man should be.

back." Phaedo, Crito, and several others began crying openly, and Apollodorus cried out loudly in a fit of despair. "What is this strange outcry?" Socrates asked. "I sent away the women just to avoid such an outburst, for I have been told that a man should die in peace. Be quiet then, and have patience."

For their mentor's sake, the younger men fought back their tears. Some of them stood at his sides as he walked around the cell, as the attendant had instructed him. When his legs became heavy and numb, they laid him on his back. Several minutes passed, during which the attendant periodically examined Socrates' feet and legs; finally, he pressed one foot quite hard and asked if the older man could feel it. "No, I cannot," Socrates answered. More mo-

*This famous painting by the eighteenth-century French artist Jacques Louis David (pronounced dah-VEED) dramatically captures the moment when Socrates prepares to drink the poison.*

ments passed, and the man pressed his legs higher up. He felt nothing there either. The cold, numbness, and stiffness were clearly working their way upward, and as all of those present realized, when the effects of the poison reached the heart, death would come.

After a few more minutes had gone by, Socrates suddenly said, "Crito, I owe a rooster to the healing god, Asclepius. Would you be so kind as to see that my debt is paid?"

"It shall be done, my friend," Crito assured him. "Is there anything else I can do?" But he received no answer. Socrates' body had become very still. A few seconds later, Crito reached over and gently closed the old man's mouth and eyes. For a long time the room remained very quiet, save for the faint sounds of weeping.

"So ended the life of our dear friend," Plato later recalled. "I can truly say that of all the men I have ever known, he was by far the best, the wisest, and the most just."

# Epilogue

# The Legacy of Socrates' Trial

T HOUGH THE TRIAL AND MARTYRDOM of Socrates were newsworthy events when they happened, they had no immediate effect on either Athenian politics and social life or Greek society in general. Athenian law and the court system were unaffected, for the event did not break any legal ground. Politics went on as usual, as evidenced by the fact that Anytus, the chief instigator of the charges against the philosopher, remained a leading and admired figure in Athens for more than a decade after the trial. Apparently there was no public revulsion over the trial and its harsh verdict during these years or for a long time afterward. Indeed, for at least a century, with the exception of Plato, Xenophon, and a few others, Greek writers hardly mentioned the trial; even the great Aristotle, Plato's pupil, who profoundly influenced later literature, philosophy, and politics, did not refer to it.

Modern scholars believe that the reason for this widespread public acceptance of the trial and its verdict was that few people at the time believed that verdict was unjust. In fact, writes I. F. Stone, "a half century after the trial of Socrates the popular view was that the old 'sophist' got what he deserved because he was the teacher of the hated Critias." That the barefoot sage had somehow influenced the equally despised Alcibiades and also that he had been a vocal critic of democracy was enough to blacken his memory for the average Greek of that era.

## Inspired by Injustice

Plato, of course, was far from average. He was a man of tremendous intellect, energy, and purpose, and his mentor's trial and martyrdom had a profound effect on him and his thinking. Socrates' condemnation and execution filled Plato with disgust, and he became disillusioned with democracy and with Athens's politics and legal

*Plato, whose writings preserved Socrates' memory and teachings for future generations.*

system. The trial and its aftermath caused the younger man to think more and more about the problems of moral and political injustice, as he indicated in this excerpt from one of his letters:

> When I considered these things and the men in charge of public affairs, and made a closer study of law and custom as I grew older, it seemed even more difficult to govern a state rightly. . . . At the same time the whole fabric of law and custom was growing worse and worse at a troubling rate. As a result, although I had been at first full of enthusiasm for a public career, when I saw all this happening . . . I was at last completely bewildered. My thoughts became preoccupied with how this situation might be changed, and especially the whole organization of the state.

Inspired by the injustice that had befallen the individual whom he had earlier called "the most just man then living," Plato went on to write about justice, law, the use and misuse of political power, and the structure of the ideal state and its government. After traveling around the Mediterranean world for some twenty years, he returned to Athens and established the Academy. The first true university in the modern sense, the school was designed as a training ground for a new breed of statesmen, in Plato's view, men of deep personal conviction, commitment to virtue and good works, and a strong sense of justice. It might be too late for his native Athens to become the ideal state, Plato reasoned, but the "philosophic rulers" he hoped to produce might eventually change the world for the better.

## The Philosopher-Saint

Plato's dream of a troubled world transforming itself into the wise and just utopia he envisioned in his famous *Republic* did not become reality. However, his writings and ideas and those of his student Aristotle had far-reaching effects on the scientists, philosophers, and religious leaders of later generations. At the same time, thanks to Plato, Greek society and the later Western societies that inherited Greece's cultural legacy eventually came to see Socrates' accusation, trial, and death as morally unjust acts. Socrates became to the general public what he had been to

Plato—a sort of philosopher-saint, the very personification of the martyr for truth who chooses death over betraying his convictions.

This moral choice Socrates exemplified later influenced a number of religious faiths, including Christianity. The idea of standing on personal conscience rather than following socially accepted but unjust laws became one of Christianity's principal tenets. Over the years many Christians martyred themselves for their beliefs, as Socrates had.

Another way that the philosopher indirectly influenced Christianity was by formulating a compelling concept of the immortal human soul. "When Christianity came to the Graeco-Roman

*A Roman mosaic from the Italian town of Pompeii portrays a gathering of philosophers at Plato's Academy.*

*Socrates' conception of the invisible and immortal human soul later became
an important element of the Christian religion.*

world," A. E. Taylor points out, "it found the general conception
of the soul which it needed already prepared for it by philosophy."
Socrates' view of the soul as invisible, eternal, and the seat of intelligence and morality became another cornerstone of Christian
thought. To the vast majority of Europeans and their descendants
around the world today, says Taylor, "the importance of the soul is
a doctrine so familiar that it seems self-evident."

# A Moral Example for the World

In a very real way, then, Socrates' martyrdom set in motion the Platonic philosophic revolution that formed the foundation for much of later Western thought. Had Socrates not been accused, convicted, and killed for his ideas, his notoriety would have been far smaller; indeed, his name might have ended up as a mere footnote in later philosophy books. Plato might have gone on to do and write a great deal, but without the example of injustice set by his friend's trial and execution, his life, ideas, and creative output would surely have been very different. Subsequent developments in Western philosophy, literature, and religion would have been different as well.

It is probable that none of what did happen as a result of Socrates's martyrdom would surprise him. He chose death not only as an expression of personal conscience but also to provide a moral example for his friends and troubled countrymen, and through them, for later generations. Believing that people would eventually learn from his sacrifice, in the final moments of his trial he told his accusers, "Many critics will one day rise up and denounce your injustice." And in the fullness of time, that prediction came true. The world came to understand and appreciate Socrates' sacrifice and to applaud and revere the qualities of unselfishness and nobility that motivated it. Xenophon perhaps said it best when he wrote of his friend:

> In contemplating the man's wisdom and nobility of character, I find it beyond my power to forget him, or, in remembering him, to refrain from praising him. And if, among those who make virtue their aim, anyone has ever been brought into contact with a person more helpful than Socrates, I count that man worthy to be called most blessed.

# For Further Reading

Jonathon Barnes, *Early Greek Philosophy*. New York: Penguin Books, 1987. An excellent general introduction to the pre-Socratic Greek thinkers who influenced Socrates and Plato. Excerpts from the works of these early philosophers are accompanied by helpful explanatory captions.

Olivia Coolidge, *The Golden Days of Greece*. New York: Thomas Y. Crowell, 1968. An easy-to-read synopsis of the main events and characters of Greece's famed Classical age with a full chapter devoted to Socrates and his importance.

Rhoda A. Hendricks, trans., *Classical Gods and Heroes*. New York: Morrow Quill, 1974. A collection of easy-to-read translations of famous Greek myths as told by ancient Greek and Roman writers, including Homer, Hesiod, Pindar, Sophocles, and Ovid. Socrates and other characters in Plato's dialogues refer to a number of these traditional ancient stories.

Don Nardo, *Ancient Greece*. San Diego: Lucent Books, 1994.

———, *Life in Ancient Greece*. San Diego: Lucent Books, 1995.

———, *The Age of Pericles*. San Diego: Lucent Books, 1996. These concise overviews offer useful general background information on the events, customs, and personalities of the unique society and era that produced the equally unique Socrates.

Susan Peach and Anne Millard, *The Greeks*. London: Usborne, 1990. A very handy general overview of the history and culture of ancient Greece, including information on how the legal system worked. Filled with excellent and accurate color illustrations.

Richard H. Popkin and Avrum Stroll, *Philosophy Made Simple*. New York: Doubleday, 1993. This very easy to read overview of the major Western philosophical concepts and trends includes sections on the contributions of Socrates and Plato.

Chester G. Starr, *The Ancient Greeks*. New York: Oxford University Press, 1971. A fine general introductory volume on ancient Greek history and culture by a noted scholar. Contains a discussion of Greek scientific and philosophical thought, how it developed, and the contributions of Socrates and Plato.

Hugh Tredennick and Harold Tarrant, trans., *The Last Days of Socrates*. New York: Penguin Books, 1993. Concise, easy-to-read translations of some of the key Plato dialogues dealing with Socrates—*Euthyphro, Apology, Crito*, and *Phaedo*.

# Works Consulted

Reginald E. Allen, *Greek Philosphy: Thales to Aristotle*. New York: Macmillan, 1985.

Alan F. Blum, *Socrates, the Original and Its Images*. London: Routledge and Kegan Paul, 1978.

C. M. Bowra, *The Greek Experience*. New York: New American Library, 1957.

Thomas C. Brickhouse and Nicholas D. Smith, *Plato's Socrates*. New York: Oxford University Press, 1994.

Will Durant, *The Life of Greece*. New York: Simon and Schuster, 1939.

Paul Edwards, ed., *The Encyclopedia of Philosophy*. 8 vols. New York: Macmillan, 1967.

Kathleen Freeman, *Ancilla to the Pre-Socratic Philosophers*. Cambridge, MA: Harvard University Press, 1970.

Charles L. Griswold Jr., ed., *Platonic Writings, Platonic Readings*. New York: Routledge, 1988.

Norman Gulley, *The Philosophy of Socrates*. New York: Macmillan, 1968.

Moses Hadas, ed., *The Complete Plays of Aristophanes*. New York: Bantam Books, 1962.

Edith Hamilton, *The Greek Way to Western Civilization*. New York: New American Library, 1942.

J. D. Kaplan, ed., *Dialogues of Plato: Apology, Crito, Phaedo, Symposium, Republic*. Translated by Benjamin Jowett. New York: Pocket Books, 1955.

Plato, *Dialogues*. 5 vols. Translated by Benjamin Jowett. Oxford: Clarendon Press, 1875.

————, *Symposium*. Translated by Tom Griffith. Berkeley: University of California Press, 1989.

Leo Rauch, *Plato's Republic and Other Works*. New York: Simon and Schuster, 1965.

Ian Scott-Kilvert, trans., *The Rise and Fall of Athens: Nine Greek Lives by Plutarch*. New York: Penguin Books, 1960.

I. F. Stone, *The Trial of Socrates*. Boston: Little, Brown, 1988.

A. E. Taylor, *Socrates: The Man and His Thought*. New York: Doubleday, 1952.

Gregory Vlastos, *Socratic Studies*. Cambridge, England: Cambridge University Press, 1994.

Gregory Vlastos, ed., *The Philosophy of Socrates: A Collection of Critical Essays*. Notre Dame, IN: University of Notre Dame Press, 1971.

Pearl C. Wilson, *The Living Socrates*. Owings Mills, MD: Stemmer House, 1975.

Xenophon, *Memorabilia of Socrates*. Boston: Allyn and Bacon, 1890.

————, *Memorabilia and Oeconimicus*. Translated by E. C. Marchant. Cambridge, MA: Harvard University Press, 1965.

# Index

# Picture Credits

Cover photo: Stock Montage, Inc.

AKG London, 83, 86

Alinari/Art Resource, NY, 10, 54

Archive Photos, 25

Corbis-Bettmann, 21 (bottom), 28, 37, 39, 48, 69, 75

Culver Pictures, 21 (top), 44, 65, 78

Erich Lessing/Art Resource, NY, 19, 31

Hulton Deutsch Collection Limited, 29, 71

Library of Congress, 8, 12, 18 (bottom), 46

North Wind Picture Archives, 13, 18 (top), 20, 33, 34, 38, 64, 74, 81

Scala/Art Resource, NY, 61, 85

Stock Montage, Inc., 57

# About the Author

Don Nardo is an award-winning author whose more than seventy books include many in his main field, the history and culture of classical Greece and Rome. In addition to this volume on the trial of Socrates and five general studies of Greek and Roman history and life, he has written *Greek and Roman Theater*, *The Battle of Marathon*, *The Age of Pericles*, *The Punic Wars*, *Caesar's Conquest of Gaul*, *The Age of Augustus*, and several others. Mr. Nardo also dabbles periodically in orchestral composition, oil painting, screenwriting, and film directing. He lives with his wife, Christine, on Cape Cod, Massachusetts.